D0722269

A READER'S GUIDE TO THE PLAYS OF W. B. YEATS

A READER'S GUIDE
TO THE PLAYS OF
W. B. YEATS

Richard Taylor

St. Martin's Press   New York

© Richard Taylor 1984

All rights reserved. For information, write:
St. Martin's Press, Inc., 175 Fifth Avenue, New York, NY 10010
Printed in Hong Kong
First published in the United States of America in 1984

ISBN 0–312–66456–7

Library of Congress Cataloging in Publication Data

Taylor, Richard, 1935–
A reader's guide to the plays of W. B. Yeats.

Bibliography:p.
Includes index.
1. Yeats, W. B. (William Butler), 1865–1939–
Dramatic works.   I. Title.
PR5908.D7T38   1982   822'.8   81–21295
ISBN 0–312–66456–7   AACR2

For Floyd and Lillian Taylor

Contents

Acknowledgements

I wish to thank Robert Welch for his help in tracking down translations of Old Irish texts and both Aina Pavolini Taylor and Robert Fox for invaluable support and help in preparing the typescript for publication.

I am grateful to M. B. Yeats, Miss Anne Yeats, Macmillan London Ltd and The Macmillan Press Ltd for permission to quote from the work of W. B. Yeats.

I am grateful to the Macmillan Publishing Co. Inc. for permission to quote from *The Variorum Edition of the Plays of W. B. Yeats*, edited by Russell K. Alspach, copyright © Russell K. Alspach and Bertha Georgie Yeats 1966; copyright © Macmillan & Co. Ltd 1965; and for permission to reproduce illustrations from *A Vision*, copyright © Macmillan & Co. Ltd 1937.

1 Introduction

The object of a reader's guide is to present the work and thought of an author as clearly and simply as possible and to help the reader to a basic understanding of the texts themselves. In the case of Yeats's plays this is not an easy task, but it is certainly not impossible. Considering the aims of the present volume, its complex subject matter and the limitations of space, there is no opportunity for either originality or comprehensiveness. One can only hope to avoid being mystifying and tedious. The individual texts will be discussed as they appear in *The Variorum Edition of the Plays of W. B. Yeats* (1966) which is based on the author's last revisions and preferred sequence of titles. Yeats rewrote many of his plays over and over again during his life-time, but in so short a work as this little attention can be paid to the various revisions and stages of development through which each passed. Because of their secondary relevance to his own creative work, the adaptations from the Greek, *Sophocles' King Oedipus* (1928) and *Sophocles' Oedipus at Colonus* (1934), are not dealt with, nor is *Fighting the Waves* (1934), a prose rewriting of *The Only Jealousy of Emer* which was not included in *The Collected Plays of W. B. Yeats* (1952). The initial dates given for the plays indicate first publication in the present revised form and not necessarily the year or order in which they were written. For purposes of comparison and clarification the date of the original publication is also supplied as well as that of the first performance during Yeats's lifetime. The table on page 2 which lists all three dates for works as ordered in the *Collected Plays*, gives a good idea of the relative chronology.

In order to create a context for the discussion of individual plays, I shall begin with an outline of basic ideas which are necessary to any reading of them. However, these should not be taken as the sum total of ideas and events which influenced Yeats's life and art. Only that material which is directly relevant to an understanding of the plays is, in fact, included. Suggestions for further reading are given in a separate section at the end of the volume.

(title)	(C.P.)	(orig. pub.)	(lst perf.)
The Countess Cathleen	1892	1892	1899
The Land of Heart's Desire	1894	1894	1894
Cathleen ni Houlihan	1902	1902	1902
The Pot of Broth	1904	1903	1902
The King's Threshold	1904	1904	1903
The Shadowy Waters	1911	1900	1904
Deirdre	1907	1907	1906
At the Hawk's Well	1917	1917	1916
The Green Helmet	1910	1910	1908
On Baile's Strand	1904	1903	1904
The Only Jealousy of Emer	1919	1919	1922
The Hour-Glass	1914	1903	1903
The Unicorn from the Stars	1908	1908	1907
The Player Queen	1922	1922	1919
The Dreaming of the Bones	1919	1919	1931
Calvary	1920	1921	—
The Cat and the Moon	1926	1924	1931
The Resurrection	1931	1931	1934
The Words upon the Window-Pane	1934	1934	1934
A Full Moon in March	1935	1935	—
The King of the Great Clock Tower	1935	1934	1934
The Herne's Egg	1938	1938	—
Purgatory	1939	1939	1938
The Death of Cuchulain	1939	1939	—

In order to avoid unnecessary confusion, I have retained Yeats's old fashioned spelling of Irish names, and because of the need for brevity, summaries of action have been included only where they are necessary to an understanding of the text. The reader's familiarity with the plays is always assumed and quotations are therefore held to a minimum. In the case of certain songs from the middle and later plays where the density of figurative language requires lengthy discussion, the reader should have the primary text at hand for easy reference.

Many readers will not be interested in every play that Yeats wrote and because of this fact, the discussion of individual plays has been made as independent and autonomous as possible. The obvious drawback of such a decision is to introduce a certain amount of unavoidable repetition, as some points have to be made over and over again. The inevitable monotony is somewhat relieved by the great diversity of subject matter and method of composition in the plays themselves. The choice and balance of material to be included in a reader's guide is, of course, problematical. I have deliberately avoided such areas of study as the various revisions, the extent of Lady Gregory's collaboration, the biographical level of the plays, etc. in the belief that help in reading and understanding specific aspects of the text is more important than repeating critical generalities readily available elsewhere. On the other hand, I have included some observations on the rhythmic structure of each play, and the patterning of images since they are both such important features of poetic composition and ones which have been too often overlooked or underestimated.

THE CONCEPT OF RITUAL DRAMA

For the beginner the most puzzling aspect of Yeats's work for the theatre is the fact that it is very different from the kind of drama one has read and studied at school. Even some of the early critics questioned Yeats's dramatic instinct and upbraided him for a lack of consuming interest in character study and detailed plot development. Of course, in saying this they had a different model in mind, but we are now beginning to acknowledge that Yeats was no less a dramatist for refusing to follow theatre tradition as it had been handed on to him. From the time of Shakespeare English drama had presented stage pictures of a more or less realistic world in which both character and event closely resembled those of every-day life. Traditional drama was essentially a narrative in which plot and its eventual outcome implied meaning, an observation, or a comment on human experience. The structure of individual plays was normally based on the interaction of characters and events as a dramatic situation was introduced to the audience, developed, reached a catastrophe or crisis and then worked itself out towards a climactic resolution or unravelling of the original conflict. Emphasis and interest centred on the delineation and development of characters as they reacted to the situations in which they found themselves, as well as on the logic and inevitability of action through which the author's theme or themes were expressed. The depth and complexity of psychological insight, social observation and philosophical speculation along with the aesthetic pleasures of plot construction were the rewarding aspects of conventional drama. But Yeats wished to create a new and different dramatic form with which to project a radically different world-view.

As a symbolist, Yeats was committed to the spiritual or metaphysical implications of the human condition rather than to the temporal or physical aspects of the individual's existence in society. Instead of producing the illusion of real or every-day experience in order to expose and comment on it, he wished to project a concrete image of universal or metaphysical forces, which, he thought, determined the human condition, in order to emphasise the living relationship between the temporal world and an antecedently spiritual universe. With its primary focus on the actual presentation of action before an audience, drama was the obvious literary form for achieving a physical image and even his earliest experiments tend to be simple metaphors acted out upon a stage in which the interaction of characters and events represents a dramatic truth about the relationship between the temporal and spiritual worlds. Of course, lyric poetry with its musical intensity and verbal imagery also provided a means of achieving his end: 'Personal utterance, which had almost ceased in English literature, could be as fine an escape from rhetoric and abstraction as drama itself. But my father would hear of nothing but drama; personal utterance was only egotism.' (Yeats, 1955, pp. 102–3) The ideal solution was to merge the incantatory effects of lyric poetry and its patterns of symbols with the objective characters, actions, and stage pictures of drama. The narrative method of conventional tragedy and comedy were replaced by the concept of ritual. Any action in real life can be turned into a ritual if it is performed with ceremonial gestures and speech inflections. Breaking bread, lighting candles, or drinking wine are perfectly ordinary acts which can be ritualised by a slight exaggeration or stylisation. Another way to ritualise an every-day act is to repeat the sequence of its parts on successive occasions in exactly the same order with identical movements and intonation, either with or without exaggeration and stylisation. Putting a child to bed or preparing one's desk for work can easily be raised to the level of ritual, and any process so institutionalised comes to represent and to ensure the inevitability as well as the effectiveness of that action. Drama itself grew out of ritual performances and Yeats wished to return to that source and inspiration in order to emphasise the correspondence between human actions and their spiritual or universal prototypes.

Ritual drama is distinguishable from other kinds of theatre in that it directs the attention of the audience towards the inevitability and representative meaning of the action rather than towards the inner conflict of tragedy or the reassertion of outward order after a comic inversion or intervention. Ritual drama is a direct presentation of inevitability, an affirmation or celebration of its necessity and rightness as in *The Bacchae* of Euripides, John Milton's *Samson Agonistes* or J. M. Synge's *Riders to the Sea*, where characterisation and action are limited in development so that attention may centre on the working out of an inescapable conclusion; the fall of Pentheus who defies the god, the apotheosis of Samson who surmounts temptation, and the transcendence of Maurya who reconciles herself to the inevitability of human mortality. Pentheus does not show right mastery of his universe while Samson and Maurya do. The ideal of control in each case is affirmed, accepted, and surrendered to by the audience as a result of participating imaginatively in the ritual performance. Rather than imitate established dramatic structures, Yeats looked for a new and non-narrative form. His early plays show evidence of both the search for a workable precedent and exciting experimentation with theoretical techniques, traditional as well as revolutionary. The two approaches later cohered into a general dramatic method which is well adapted to the ritualisation of his subject matter. More often than not a single incident is involved rather than a complex plot sequence and the action is already familiar to the audience as it derives from traditional myth, legend, or ritual. Attention is therefore drawn away from the psychology of the characters and the outcome of action in order to concentrate on the way in which that action works itself out to an already accepted and inevitable end. The form of the drama itself and its projection of the relationship between the temporal and spiritual worlds is nearly always the centre of interest in Yeats's plays. There is no established form or traditional design for the action of ritual drama, and, in fact, very few pure examples of the genre exist. Usually, we find that there are ritual elements or qualities in plays which are normally classified under other headings; history plays and tragedies in particular. Yeats needed an alternative structure if he were to write ritual drama as distinct from conventional plot oriented plays, and at first he tried simple, dramatic conflicts in one-act structures which were resolved by the direct intervention of supernatural forces. The one-act play was then in vogue, as was the newly conceived short story, and its brief intensity of construction was sometimes combined in Yeats's early plays with the structural features of classical Greek tragedy and/or the treatment of character and situation as derived from medieval mystery or morality plays.

Cultural authority was also invoked through the use of subject matter derived from Irish folk material, legend and heroic myth. Yeats's conception of theatre was as much ethnic as metaphysical and he also wished to celebrate the political and moral ideals of Celtic Ireland as well as his own spiritual aspirations. In the beginning the national theatre which he helped to found looked to the Irish peasantry for its inspiration, since they were presumed to be the guardians of a purely Celtic culture, but Yeats himself turned more and more to the authority of the heroic myths of the ancient Gaelic people whose culture had been debased by alien conquest and colonisation.

In place of the multiplicity of characters and events which provide interest and variety in full-length narrative drama, Yeats relied on the various techniques of stage production which were then being exploited as part of the revival of theatre art. At first he experimented with music, song, rhythmic movement and dance, as additional means of expression. He spent a good deal of time devising methods of speaking or chanting verse for maximum effectiveness. Yeats was greatly interested in stage pictures and gave much attention to the design of the playing area, costumes, properties, scenery and lighting, especially emphasising their symbolic or representative nature. In all these efforts he was attempting to resolve the then-current question of illusionism: Should a play create the illusion of an actual and viable reality or of a self-conscious and explicitly imaginative existence? Should the audience be distanced or isolated from whatever reality was created on stage or should the barrier between audience and action be broken down once and for all? Above everything, Yeats was a man of the theatre who conceived of his plays as larger enterprises than mere literary texts. In order to appreciate the potency and force of his brief rituals for the stage, it is necessary to imagine them as actual performances. A good deal of the stylisation which gives them their ritual quality is to be found in the hieratic gestures, voice rhythms, movement, costumes, and stage settings of an actual production. Yeats never did evolve a settled dramatic form which he then adhered to, rather he combined and recombined selected constructional features and elements of production method in various ways throughout his career. In order to follow out this argument, however, it is best to discuss the peculiar qualities of individual plays one by one.

THE USES OF MAGIC

As in his lyric poetry, there is a striking congruity between the form or scheme of ritual action in Yeats's plays and the conception of reality which they exemplify, a coincidence of the arcane or esoteric wisdom he wished to communicate and the aesthetic forms through which he expressed them. The key to this achievement is found in his understanding of magic talismans; that is, images, symbols or rituals which operate by exact correspondence with the workings of a spiritual universe after which they are patterned. The idea is that the spiritual universe requires temporal existence and casts downwards for its images, dreams and visions, just as the temporal world requires the spiritual and casts upwards for illumination and the reconciliation of contradictions. Each needs the other in order to complete or fulfil itself. By creating a pattern or scheme of relationships which echoes the design or dynamics of the spiritual universe, one can call its power into action and so penetrate the barrier between the two worlds. Magic talismans act indirectly by invoking parallel moods, influences, and even circumstances which inevitably bring the separate worlds of spirit and nature closer together. 'The central principle of all the Magic of power is that everything we formulate in the imagination, if we formulate it strongly enough, realises itself in the circumstances of life, acting either through our own souls, or through the spirits of nature.' (Yeats, 1974, p. 265) Occult teaching of the late nineteenth century held fast to the neo-platonic idea that the visible universe was the proportional measure of the invisible and pretended to mediate between the physical forms of nature and that universal force whose furthest manifestations they were, by meditating on the unbroken chain of cause and effect which united them.

> The doctrine of universal analogy as the basis of progressive revelation is a noble and beautiful hypothesis which eminently recommends itself to reason, and once properly understood, it would be an inexhaustible fountain of purest inspiration for the poetry of the age to come; it transfers the whole visible universe into one grand symbol, and the created intelligence of man

becomes a microcosmic god whose facilities are in exact though infinitesimal proportion with the uncreated and eternal mind. Apart from direct revelation, it would be truly 'the sole possible mediator between the seen and the unseen,' establishing the grounds of faith in the rationality of a single assumption, and harmonising the positivism of physical science with the religion of legitimate aspirations towards the infinity of the unknown. (Waite, 1886, pp. xxxi–ii)

Given the doctrine of correspondences and the effectiveness of imagination, there need be no distinction between a magical rite and a ritual drama which might also chart the pattern of spiritual reality and present a metaphorical image of it.

Yeats spent a good deal of his life trying to map out the patterns of spiritual reality and wrote a number of serious prose essays attempting to construct a system which would help him to concentrate the complexities and oppositions of all experience into a single metaphor. The second edition of *A Vision* (1937) contains the final version of his ideas, his view of history, human personality and the universal forces which determine man's existence and experience. The material in that work is of some importance to the serious and committed student of Yeats, especially to anyone interested in the lyric poetry, since a number of direct references to its imagery are contained in Yeats's verse. Outside of an understanding of its basic concept or principle, however, a particular knowledge of the system outlined in *A Vision* is not altogether necessary to a reading of the plays. A very clear explanation of Yeats's principal images, the gyre and the great wheel, is given in the introduction to *A Reader's Guide to William Butler Yeats* (1959) by John Unterecker, and there is not much point in repeating it here in its entirety. Let it suffice to say that the underlying mechanism of the system is activated by conflict and opposition. Every aspect of human personality and historical epochs has an essential character or identifiable nature which both conflicts with and seeks to reconcile itself with its exact opposite. Just as the natural and supernatural worlds attract and repel one another, so do the various different aspects of people and periods of time. Yeats believed that all human or temporal activity is in a constant state of movement between the extremes of primary (objective, solar, active, or reasonable) and antithetical (subjective, lunar, creative, or emotional) being. If, for instance, a near-complete and perfect primary state of being could be achieved, then that person or culture would naturally develop towards its own opposite, its objectivity diminishing as its new subjectivity increases. Yeats imagined this movement as the progress of a point spiralling from the base of a cone to its top or from the top to its base. He called the figure a gyre. In order to show the interpenetration of primary and antithetical states, their complementary relationship at all stages, he often showed his gyres or cones in an interlocking position.

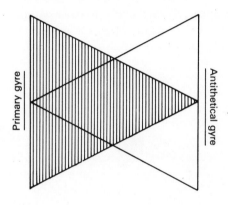

In this single figure Yeats created a convenient diagram or scheme by which to measure the quality of characters in an individual or culture at any given point in time, the exact combination of opposed characteristics present at any one moment. One's nature might be predominantly primary while only slightly antithetical or vice versa. One might be wholly at one end of the scale or the other, and the final possibility is to find one's nature exactly at the mid-point between the extremes and so incapable of either physical action or intellectual decision.

The great wheel is an elaboration of the gyre metaphor which names and identifies twenty-eight phases or positions along the interpenetrating cones and arranges them into a circle in order to emphasise the cyclical progression of characteristics which men and societies pass through in their natural efforts to realise their full potential and merge with their own opposites. The scheme is obviously based on astrological principles but rather than the twelve signs of the zodiac, it exploits the waxing and waning of the moon whose full and dark phases are perfect images of lunar and solar natures respectively. The metaphor is a good deal more complex and detailed than so brief a description implies, but complete and detailed knowledge of the system is not absolutely necessary to an understanding of the plays.

Like the image of interlocking gyres, the great wheel is relevant to human experience on several different planes. It can be taken to represent the basic phases in the life of a single individual or of a society, as well as the dominant characteristics of successive incarnations and historical ages which make up the larger cycles of human existence. At one level a man or woman may be said to experience all twenty-eight phases between birth and death (phases 1 and 15, of course, in a spiritual existence only).

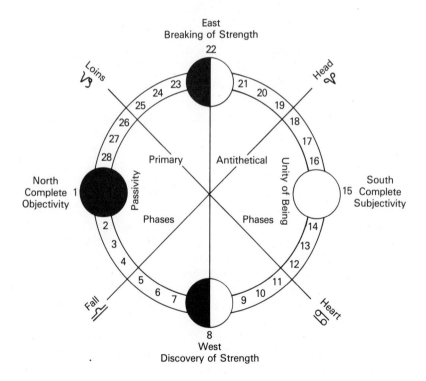

On another, a dominant characteristic may also place them in a single phase of a larger cycle for that lifetime. Presumably the next incarnation will find them at a succeeding stage on the great wheel, and so it is with historical periods which take about two thousand years for each full cycle to complete itself. Once the great wheel has been circled, a succeeding cycle which has an opposite or antithetical nature is entered upon and the whole process is begun again.

As Yeats worked out his ideas of universal order with more and more precise detail, his ritual dramas reflected the various patterns and interrelationships of the visionary systems he was constructing. The characters he portrayed and their motives as well as the actions and their outcomes exemplified, and therefore represented, the inner workings of the universe. Each play became a talisman through which one can appreciate some aspect of universal order and through which spiritual forces energise themselves in the temporal world.

Scholars and critics have never been altogether comfortable with such strange and unorthodox ideas. Attempts have actually been made to argue that Yeats was basically a Christian and did not really believe in all the esoteric doctrines which he so ardently studied throughout a long and active lifetime. One should remember that Yeats was brought up in an age of agnosticism which followed both the confirmation of scientific method in Darwin's *On the Origin of Species* (1859) and the disillusionment of late Victorian times in materialism and progress. Scientific idealism suggested that the personal god of the Old Testament, who had created the universe at a single blow, must give way to ideas of a more abstract, universal force whose furthest manifestations are physical forms. Similarly, the god of the New Testament was not easily reconcilable with the unspeakable social realities of the industrial revolution. Like many other individuals of that time Yeats could no longer believe in a formal or conventional Christianity. In both folklore and mystical–occult disciplines such as Platonism, cabalistic studies, oriental philosophy and theurgic magic, he encountered an active spirituality which existed both outside of and within man, linking him by an unbroken chain of being to an ultimate spiritual reality. Out of these ideas Yeats constructed a system, not itself reality, but the pattern of reality. It was a stylised arrangement of experience by which he, as an individual with a given nature and needs peculiar to himself, might hold both reality and justice in a single thought. Yeats's ideas of religion and philosophy are not in themselves of consuming importance, but they are interesting in so far as they give rise to the expressive forms and passionate content of his poems and plays.

In addition to the concept of verse drama as a structural symbol or magic talisman based on the metaphor of gyre and great wheel, some of the middle and later plays also include actions or situations which exemplify the doctrine of dreaming back. Yeats was very interested in spiritualism and explained the existence of ghosts and other supernatural manifestations as projections of imagination by the spirits of the dead whose heightened passions and attachment to life were so strong that they dreamed back through their past experiences. They might even dream back over and over again until they were purged of remorse and memory, freed to continue to the next stage of the cycle. Images of such spirits projected as mummies, bobbins or perns (gyres) unwinding the bands or threads of experience from about themselves are familiar from such poems as 'Byzantium' and 'All Souls' Night'. In the plays there many examples of supernatural intervention as some dead soul dreams back compulsively and so projects a concrete and passionate presence or scene into the temporal world.

THE DOCTRINE OF PERSONALITY AND MASK

Personality and passion are key concepts in the study of Yeats's plays, for it is the experience of an intensely passionate moment in the life of a character which gives those rituals their dramatic quality and power. Characters usually find themselves in situations of conflict or out of harmony with the forces around them, and they seek a more congenial or fulfilling mode of existence. The choice and decision may either be conscious or abruptly thrust upon them by universal (spiritual) forces manifesting themselves in the physical world. The dramatic action of the plays centres on the transformation of character from one state to another, a transmutation of personality through an ecstasy of passion which both purifies and ennobles.

Yeats, himself, was a subjective, introspective, and creative man who admired all those qualities which he did not possess: objectivity, physical force, and moral assertion. He did not wish to lose his proper identity but rather to embrace or encompass those aspects of character which were most unlike his own. If such opposites could be reconciled; that is, integrated and unified in a single personality, then that individual would be in complete control of his world and fully responsible for his own destiny. As Yeats developed his ideas into a universal vision of confrontation and integration, he came to use the word 'mask' to refer to that ideal opposition or image which would generate a creative and satisfying tension. Rather than an artificial image behind which the real personality might hide, the Yeatsian mask is an imaginary condition or state of being to be achieved in order to integrate all possibilities into an individual's personal experience. It is through the creative tension between character and mask that the individual gains completeness of personality and command of the world around him. In the same way, such an enlargement of personality is also a step towards developing a personal or mystical relationship with the active supernatural forces of the universe. Yeats also believed that a relationship exists between the individual and his or her daimon, a spirit double or guide, something like a guardian angel, which emanates from the spiritual world. The daimon is also activated by a desire for completion through integration or union with both its spiritual and temporal opposite. As we have seen, Yeats understood all human experience as a warring of opposites, a continuous alternation, while the concepts of mask and daimon provided an external form or image by which the process might be expressed.

In the plays, Yeats is primarily interested in showing characters who are more or less identifiable by personality type or aspiration and who are engaged in interaction with either mask, daimon, or both. In the later plays, especially, the mask or daimon is often personified, a separate character whose relationship with the other figures of the drama is a paradigm of Yeats's philosophical dialectics. Of course, the characters in the plays are essentially human, they are differentiated and developed to one degree or another, but their representative nature within the symbolic scheme of action is more important still. In Yeats's lyric poetry, on the other hand, real people, his friends and contemporaries, are celebrated and raised to the level of symbols because of the ennobling transformation they had undergone through their intense and passionate lives. By now we are all familiar with Lionel Johnson and John O'Leary, George Pollexfen and Maud Gonne, J. M. Synge and Major Robert Gregory. Each of them had developed either towards complete spirituality and withdrawal into the self or towards total physicality and participation in the world outside the self. In the plays, however, we find representative types and figures from legend, myth or history. Instead of the supposedly real and physical world of conventional narrative drama, Yeats gives us a symbolic representation of an ideal pattern, an actual stage image of an abstraction. He even carried his philosophical dialectics to the point of developing a style of acting, speaking, and stage decor which is the anti-self of traditional dramatic techniques. The production method constitutes a formal austerity or mask which expresses the intensely passionate experiences that transform the protagonists. The plays are ritual projections of human actions and experience in which the central figure reaches out to another state of being, a more intimate realisation of the antithetical condition within itself and therefore a more intimate awareness of universal order. By presenting human action as a dramatic ritual, the process of becoming is turned into a symbol, a perfected image of at least one aspect of universal order.

The development of heroic personality through the dialectic theory of masks is basic to Yeats's plays, whether applied to a character who is impelled to direct intervention in the world of physical existence or to inner fulfilment in the spiritual world as perceived through imagination. The object of the individual's natural quest in life is to comprehend experience and merge the self into an ideal unity of being, an imaginary state, perhaps best expressed through art, in which all contradictions of the human condition are resolved and reconciled. Unity of being is nothing less than the perfect balance and annihilation of consciousness between the opposing forces which determine our existence and between which man endlessly moves. It is a phase of perfect subjectivity (creativity) at the culmination of the antithetical gyre and is represented by the full moon. All other phases are taken to be stages in the progress towards or away from this optimum condition. For this reason Yeats's central characters often find themselves at either a crisis of self-identification in which they must choose between opposed aspects of their natures and desires, or at the end of their lives, having completed their characters in that incarnation and awaiting the transition to a new and opposite state of being.

The more interesting and problematical of the two situations is the first of them since a wrong choice may be made and the future

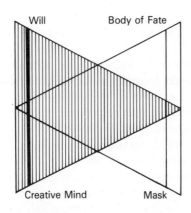

development of personality for that character subverted. Instead of being ennobled or apotheosised and thereby transcending the incompleteness of the human condition, a character might fall away from the true path to unity of being. Of the four given variables which move along the lines of the schematic representation, a certain amount of choice is open to the individual. One must will to become or embrace one's own opposite or mask; one must create, consciously and imaginatively, one's fate or destiny. As the gyre or cone made up of will and creative mind trails off into nothingness, the opposite cone of mask and body of fate takes over and becomes dominant. Interaction with a true and proper mask is no more inevitable in Yeats's system than interaction with true and proper creative mind. It is always possible to choose a false mask or mode of creativity and so fail to fulfil one's character. And even if true mask and creative mind are assumed, an individual may be moving away from unity of being, having already passed that perfect state of complete subjectivity (moon) and progressing towards complete objectivity (sun). Since the ecstatic moment for both protagonist and audience is the recognition of the relationship between individuality and its goal, unity of being, there are very definite possibilities for falling away from the ideal which, however catastrophic, ought not to be thought of in terms of conventional tragedy.

THE REDEFINITION OF TRAGEDY

There has been nearly as much speculation about Yeats's concept of tragedy as there has been about his religio–philosophical convictions, and the heart of the controversy is the question of orthodox form and interpretation. From the classical Greek period to the nineteenth century, tragedy has continued as a theatrical form in which an individual of heroic stature finds him or herself in a situation which works on a flaw in an otherwise noble character and results in a downfall which is unquestionably justified but contains some redemptive element; a recognition of personal error, an assumption of responsibility or some other re-affirmation of the original heroic stature. Tragedy has always been concerned with inner conflict, the psychology of important individuals as they operate in constricting circumstances. Tragedy demonstrates the possibility of transcending fate, of rising above the normal failings and petty conditions or limitations which threaten us. Modern tragedy, as distinct from the classical, begins with the work of such dramatists as Henrik Ibsen (1828–1906) and Maurice Maeterlinck (1862–1949), whose visions of tragedy do not include the redemptive or transcendent fall of a noble figure. In modern tragedy the individual is not generally of heroic stature, and even when this is the case, he or she is rendered helpless and ultimately frustrated by the determining realities of either a socio-economic system or the blind forces of an unremitting and inescapable supernatural order. Modern tragedy sees man as being victimised by fate rather than capable of heroic transcendence and accordingly, it has developed characteristic modes of stage presentation to project that vision. On the one hand there is the illusionistic realism of a box set and a naturalistic acting style behind a proscenium arch which constitutes a transparent fourth wall through which the 'reality' beyond is viewed. On the other, we have an open area stage with abstract or symbolic scenery as well as stylised and artificial acting technique which requires the active and imaginative participation of the audience.

Although Yeats was drawn to the modern and symbolic mode of theatrical presentation, he was steadfastly old-fashioned in his insistence on heroic transcendence, on the noble stature of his characters. But instead of the logical narrative and redemptive downfall of traditional tragedy, Yeats concentrated on the passionate moment of personal crisis and the obligation of his protagonists to will their own fate, actively bringing it into being and embracing whatever sacrifices might be necessary for its sake. In Yeats's view of reality, will and fate are more or less fixed according to the circumstances of an individual's birth, but in order to attain heroic stature, the individual must develop the potential of personality through conscious interaction with all that is opposite to his or her own character. Consciously or unconsciously, the individual chooses those qualities of the anti-self and of creativity which will fulfil that personality and lead to either control and dominance of the world or ineffectiveness and subjugation, to either transcendence or defeat. Rather than the traditional responses of pity and fear, Yeats's tragedy evokes both a welcome reassurance through the inevitability of future dialectic development even in defeat, and a joyful ecstasy through the symbolic embodiment of the highest ideals and feelings of mankind in heroic transcendence. Tragic joy or ecstasy is experienced by the audience in the passionate moment of transcendence as well as in the transmutation of individual human action into an artistic symbol. Ecstasy and joy are fundamental to the consummation of heroic character, the individual merging with his or her opposite. And in the same way, they are basic to the consummation of the perfected symbol, the play itself, which balances its dialectically opposed images and actions in such a way as to reconcile them. 'Tragedy must always be a drowning and breaking of the dykes that separate man from man, and . . . it is upon these dykes comedy keeps house.' (Yeats, 1961, p. 241)

In his effort to be encyclopaedic, to embrace or encompass all human experience, Yeats paid a good deal of attention to comedy as a natural counterpart to tragedy. Comedy is a complementary aesthetic form and Yeats found an historical precedent for juxtaposing the two, both in the ancient Greek theatre and later in classical Japanese tradition. In each case comedies were used as a contrast to the nobility and idealism of the tragic vision. Generally, comedy encourages an amused detachment from the trivial and ignoble, exposes human frailty through ridicule, and reassures us that order and justice prevail by demonstrating that both inversion and inflation are recognised and righted. While tragedy is concerned with complex characterisation and human psychology, comedy usually concentrates on representative types and complex situations or action. As he had in the case of tragedy, Yeats tended to redefine the genre to suit his own purpose. Ultimately, he developed a concept of comedy which was an ironic counterpart of his tragic vision. The poet-tramp as protagonist is an ironic inversion of the mythic hero. Through comedy, Yeats often gained distance and detachment from the intense seriousness of his esoteric ideas while playfulness and self-mockery allow audiences to entertain his vision of universal order without being asked to accept it as actual or real.

Yeats's exotic world-view, his predilection for magic and symbolism, was further balanced and made relevant to social reality by his involvement in Irish nationalism. Just as the individual approaches his or her full potential by developing towards unity of being, Yeats believed that a nation or people could only fulfil its potential by achieving unity of culture. The ancient unity of Irish culture had long since been destroyed by the intervention of an alien conqueror and the superimposition of a foreign language, values, mores, and customs. The structure of middle-class and urban society, its economics, religion, aesthetics, and practical life, had become thoroughly anglicised. In order to wrest its independence from Great Britain, Yeats believed that Ireland would have to cultivate a distinctive identity. It would have to return to its roots and recreate its personality, harmonising the contradictions and inconsistencies of its national life. For Yeats, a national theatre was the key to unity of culture and drama was an effective means through which Ireland and history could fulfil themselves. In the first place drama is a public art form and audiences can be created which cut across class barriers, depending on the accessibility, relevance to life, and dramatic force of both the play and its production. Yeats, however, was not so much a political or social activist as he was a romantic idealist, and however much he sought to base his work for the theatre in the cultural reality of Ireland, it was almost always an imagined or idealised reality rather than actual life experience to which he appealed. More often than not, even that was then reshaped and reinterpreted according to the ideas and dialectical pattern which he believed governed the universe.

In Ireland at that time there still existed a Celtic peasantry whose culture had been relatively undisturbed by the Anglo-Saxon overlords. Even their speech in English retained the musical inflections and often the syntax of Gaelic, while their imaginative life and values, their lore and literary traditions, were still related in many ways to the antique past, although that relationship had already been somewhat distorted as a result of conversion to Christianity in the fifth century. It was to them, to their lives and legends, that the early dramatists of the Irish National Theatre turned for subject matter. Yeats, however, idealised the peasantry and especially their close relationship with a supernatural world. At first he showed some interest in folk legends and beliefs as a basis for presenting a spiritual alternative to temporal existence, but a growing preoccupation with heroic stature and passionate tragedy soon turned his attention to the Celtic myth cycles of pre-Christian Ireland. Here were examples of passionate will freely creating personal fate, of ideal and heroic actions which transcended the frailties and limitations of the human condition. The heroic tales of the Red Branch (Ulster) cycles provided archetypal and dramatic images for contemplation whereby a society might rise to unity of culture. Unfortunately, however, Yeats did not understand that by radically changing the essentials of the major myths and legends he used, he was confusing and misleading his audience. By substituting the trappings of a quasi-philosophical system and conflicts involved in completing or not completing one's character for the actual values and goals of ancient Ireland, Yeats alienated both nationalists and a popular audience. At the same time the revival of those myths and legends, even in their radically altered forms, did make a contribution to national consciousness and identity. The actual features of the Irish landscape were so often celebrated in the plays and so closely associated with a cultural past as to render them powerful images and evocations of that past. Yeats used patterns of such images as structural features in many of the plays believing that such a unity of image might lead audiences to perceive the desired unity of culture by means of which society could complete or fulfil itself.

Unity of image is at least as difficult a term to define as unity of being or unity of culture, and like the concept of tragic joy or ecstasy, it is central to an understanding of Yeats's plays. Unity of image refers to the means whereby the central myths and rituals of an ethnic group are assimilated into a newly created form or interpretation which can then be handed down as a living aspect of inherited tradition. Unity of image refers to the construction of ritual drama according to the principles of a lyric poem, a tight composition of concrete images which are bound together and charged with an intense musical or rhythmic effect. The characters and situations as well as the stage properties and symbols which may be either visible or evoked through language, are patterned within a lyrical structure rather than a logical progression of action to emphasise the passionate transcendence which is the point of the performance.

IMAGE, SYMBOL, AND STYLE

Yeats saw each of his poems and plays as an organic whole or architectural structure. Students of his work are commonly invited to approach individual poems or plays as they relate to or form part of his entire output which is often taken to be a single work of art. The organic unity of the lyric poetry is perhaps more readily apparent than that of the drama, but this is largely a result of the extended and complex structure of each play as opposed to the intense brevity of individual poems. In poetry, themes and image patterns are immediately obvious while in drama they are neither so clearly stated nor so prominent. Plays require the creation of characters who reveal the qualities or states they represent through their relationships and actions. The kind of importance that repeated imagery assumes in lyric poetry is necessarily curtailed in drama. The birds and beasts, stones, streams, trees, towers and swords of the poems also appear in the plays, but more often than not in secondary or supporting roles. Those which can be represented visually and prominently on stage are often the most effective. The kind of verbal image which provides a substantive core of sign values as well as association with other contexts and deeper meaning has its place in Yeats's plays, but it is the tangible, visible stage image which tends to carry stronger implications because it functions as an independent character. Poetic or verbal imagery evokes a sensual response in the imagination of the reader, but drama is a physical and actual presentation; the object itself must either be physically there or strongly suggested through mime in order to carry its full weight of significance in the visible action of the play. By comparison, mere verbal images remain largely decorative and descriptive.

In poetry an image can be raised to the level of symbol by association with a variety of contexts and nuances of meaning until that single image comes to represent and evoke the entire cluster of ideas and interrelationships of meaning which have been brought into being by the poem. Such an image may acquire this kind of significance on being repeated and utilised in many different poems over a long period of time or the symbol may be specifically created within a single work as, for example, the images of stone and stream in Yeats's 'Easter 1916'. Images which become a familiar feature of an author's work are already well on their way to becoming symbols because each new encounter carries with it the recollection and associations of past usage as well as meaning. Many of Yeats's more common poetic images find their way into his plays, but their mere presence does not necessarily affect the symbolic significance of the action. Even representative settings and stage properties such as the ship in *The Shadowy Waters* or the burning brazier and chessboard of *Deirdre*, for example, are invested with more than their obvious metaphorical value by their direct relationship to characters, actions and ideas within the play.

The structured symbols which Yeats made of his plays rely upon the integration of all their elements to produce meaning. It was not just a question of harmonising lighting, stage design, costuming, and acting technique with the action and theme of the play, but rather of producing a composite representative image of the idea to be expressed. The jargon of symbolist theory is rather complex and confusing, but the goal was exactly the same as T. S. Eliot's objective correlative, Wyndham Lewis's vortex, or Ezra Pound's imagism.

> All sounds, all colours, all forms, either because of their preordained energies or because of long association, evoke indefinable and yet precise emotions, or, as I prefer to think, call down among us certain disembodied powers, whose footsteps over our hearts we call emotions; and when sound,

and colour, and form are in a musical relation, a beautiful relation to one another, they become, as it were, one sound, one colour, one form, and evoke an emotion that is made out of their distinct evocations and yet is one emotion. The same relation exists between all portions of every work of art, whether it be an epic or a song, and the more perfect it is, and the more various and numerous the elements that have flowed into its perfections, the more powerful will be the emotion, the power, the god it calls among us. (Yeats, 1961, pp. 156–7)

In his plays Yeats not only integrated the visible elements of stage production with action and theme but he also harmonised production method with the literary qualities of the text. Verbal images or symbols, verse rhythms and musical intervals were all brought to bear on characters and situations which themselves constituted an entire world, a microcosm or symbol of reality. The characteristic situations as well as the language used to express them are of primary importance. Over and over again we find such archetypal oppositions as good versus evil, youth versus age, male versus female, and man versus god coupled with a variety of effective verbal structures which create various kinds of symbols or schematic designs and represent some aspect of universal order.

The musical relation of parts to each other in any one of Yeats's plays is as much a question of verse composition as it is of a performance's speed or rhythm. Yeats developed several different styles and combined them in various ways with other dramatic elements to achieve different effects and tonalities. In the early plays we find both a peasant dialect which is slightly stylised but acceptably realistic, and a more impassioned, richly poetic speech which ennobles its speakers and properly belongs to a state of dream or reverie. Both styles of dramatic speech make much use of an imagery which reinforces the nature and quality of the particular world that is brought into being, that reality being further heightened or illuminated by the intervention of intensely lyrical songs on the one hand or supernatural apparitions on the other. The songs mark off, and comment on, the progress of the action. They serve as structural features as well as introduce another level of artistic activity and lead the audience to accept a ritual initiation or enchantment, which itself is not so much expressed through language as by music, dance, or stage symbol.

As Yeats turned to the heroic matter of Celtic mythology, he experimented more and more with conventional iambic pentameters in a contemporary idiom which led to a formality and seriousness of style combined with a fluent naturalness of expression. Traditional heroic speech could also be played off against dialect, and impassioned lyricism with its rich, verbal imagery might be reserved for choral interludes and songs which cause the audience to reflect or meditate on the action. At the same time, songs and choral interludes contrast with the direct symbolism of ritual gestures, wordless dances and other visible or audible theatrical images. In his desire to approximate musical composition Yeats introduced antithetical verbal styles in several of his dramas for the purpose of distinguishing the heightened significance of certain scenes or levels of existence and contrasting them with the main action and its heroic verse form. Towards the end of his career the formal iambic pentameters became more and more adapted to the flexibility and phrasing of contemporary usage; verse lines became shorter and more irregular, diction was sharper and more natural, while the musical quality was more intense and forceful than ever. In so far as language is concerned, Yeats had certainly evolved a flexible instrument for his particular kind of verse drama and he had gone a long way towards creating a new dramatic form, a new concept of dramatic construction and stage presentation which we now recognise as a stage in the development of what is called the Theatre of the Absurd.

2 Early Plays

THE COUNTESS CATHLEEN (1892)

Original Publication: London and Boston, 1892
First Performance: Dublin 1899

This play occupies a unique place among Yeats's work for the theatre in that he returned to it again and again, rewriting and revising it more often than any of his other plays. Yeats first came across the subject matter while collecting folk material for *Fairy and Folk Tales of the Irish Peasantry* (1888), but he later discovered that it had come originally from Léo Lespès *Les Matinées de Timothé Trimm* (1865). The plot is a simple story of Christian piety and the triumph of charity in a straight contest with the forces of evil. During a famine the Devil contrives to remove all possibility of alleviating the people's suffering. His followers, disguised as merchants, offer to buy souls, but the countess sells her own to ransom theirs. In every revision, however, Yeats enlarged upon the theme as well as the significance of the action by insisting on wider and more detailed symbolism. Instead of the original peasant–poet, Kevin, who adores the idealised countess, a courtly poet–hero, Aleel, figures in each scene of the final version. Cathleen's desire to act in the world outside herself and fulfil her duty towards her fellow men is balanced by Aleel's desire to subdue her active will and draw her into a subjective and ideal anarchy of the spirit. The countess is a personification of Ireland and Aleel may have been inspired by the legendary poet Aileel and his unrequited love for Queen Maeve, but the ideological opposition between poet and countess is a purely Yeatsian invention. In the same way the theme of heroic renunciation which moves characters towards disinterested purity is also a radical departure from Yeats's sources.

The countess is certainly more of an archetypal figure than a real person. She is an unquestioned representative of noble goodness, incapable of baseness or even of temptation. After actually selling her soul, she remains morally pure and an angelic apparition ends the play by announcing her joyous reception in heaven. From the very moment Cathleen enters the cottage of Shemus Rua there is no doubt of her physical and moral perfection. Her nobility and that of Aleel are emphasised by comparison and contrast with the peasantry and especially with the particularised characters of Mary and Shemus Rua. Cathleen and Mary have the quality of disinterested goodness in common and the parallelism is made abundantly clear in the final scene of act one which is played out in the theatrical presence of Mary's corpse. The actual buying of souls takes place before the bier of one who preferred to starve rather than submit to that ultimate debasement. Cathleen's triumph over evil through conscious self-sacrifice is the active counterpart to Mary's passivity. In each instance the women elect their fate. With full knowledge of the implications they proceed to act against immediate self-interest and in pursuance of an ideal. Mary's conduct leads to a justifiable and honourable death; that of the countess, to a miraculous and unforeseen apotheosis. Mary saves herself, Cathleen saves her fellow men and her sacrifice is transformed into beatitude.

The countess is more than a figurative representation of a spiritual ideal set in opposition to a debasing materialism and poverty of imagination, however. Her noble beauty is certainly an indication of her nature. As Castiglione, whom Yeats later read and admired, put it: 'beauty springs from God and is like a circle, the centre of which is goodness.' (1967, p. 330) But her being is more than just a physical manifestation of perfect goodness. She is an active principle which cannot rest so long as others are less perfect or less complete than herself and capable of being saved. It does not matter that the peasants for whom she willingly sacrifices herself are petty and corrupt as both the easy capitulation of Shemus Rua and Teigue and the satirical exposure of representative individuals by the merchants when bargaining for their souls, makes perfectly clear. In terms of Yeats's system Cathleen represents the completed personality of a primary phase and her relationship with Aleel provides the basis for that deduction.

As poet and lover, Aleel is a creative and subjective presence. He performs no other action in the fictional world of the play but to make love to Cathleen and praise her beauty. In the scene at the precise centre of the drama he prostrates himself before her, imploring her to leave the dangers of the wood in which she lives and flee with him to the protection of those who walk invisible and have foreseen the coming crisis. In a vision Aengus, the Celtic god of youth, beauty and poetry, had visited his counterpart in the physical world, and through Aleel he now suggests love and poetic insight as a substitute for self-sacrifice and the expiation of sin which obtain in the material or Christian world. Cathleen recognises Aleel's nobility of spirit and intellect, but steels her heart against his love. She renounces the symbolic union of opposites and fruition of a universal pattern in order to complete her own character and exert her influence for good in the material world. Aleel implies that Aengus is perhaps angelical and attempts to merge the old heroic world of the passionate, proud heart with the new dispensation, but the countess will have none of it. She dedicates her heart to the Christian heaven from which she expects salvation for herself and her people.

Aleel is the only character in the play who speaks of the old gods of pre-Christian Ireland and he is fully associated with their subjective, heroic and creative attributes. Through repeated references to the classical mythology of the Celtic peoples and Cathleen's obsessive Christianity, we begin to see that the basic conflict of the drama includes the opposition of the two historical ages. Perhaps the heaviest accumulation of mythic imagery occurs during Aleel's epic lament for the countess and her Christ-like sacrifice, yet even there we find some admixture of Christian references. He speaks of Balor, the Irish chimaera who is released by the submission of the countess to evil, as attended by demons, of Conchubar whom 'Hell first took hold upon/ When he killed Naoise and broke Deirdre's heart' (Yeats, 1966, p. 155) and later of 'a host heat of the blood made sin' (p. 157) which follows the sorceress Orchil upon the visionary scene. As it happens, the poetic vision is soon followed by the actual apparition of an angelic figure who announces Cathleen's salvation. While the countess moves towards the zenith of her strength, her perfect sacrifice and final apotheosis, Aleel and the world he represents is eclipsed, rendered powerless and ineffectual, except for the lyricism and imagery he infuses into the action.

Scenes one, two and four each contain a characteristic song by Aleel, while scenes three and five have his passionate and highly lyrical outbursts of love and lamentation. His first song, 'Were I but crazy for love's sake' (pp. 23 and 25), is an insolent piece of defiance directed at Shemus Rua, his opposite and anti-self. Where the countess and Mary are complementary, Aleel and Shemus are contrasts. The passionate, great-hearted poet mocks the meanness of the peasant's nature. Aleel's second song is much gayer and more light-hearted. It is a dancing song, 'Lift up the white knee' (pp. 57 and 59), and is used to dispel Cathleen's depression and fatigue on the journey home after caring for her stricken people. The short, intense poetic lines and the images of dancing and love reinforce the contrast between the sorrows of the material-rational world and the joys of the heroic-imaginative alternative which he advances at the beginning of scene three. The song in scene four is a response to Cathleen's rejection of his love and leads to lamentation over her sacrifice in the final scene. Its theme is obvious from the opening line, 'Impetuous heart, be still, be still' (p. 129), and like the very brief scene in which it features, the song seems to be born of a structural necessity rather than an organic or narrative one. It represents a stage in the emotional outline of the action just as the setting of that scene represents a stage in a similarly symmetrical scheme: cottage, wood, castle, *wood*, cottage. The epic lament of scene five returns us to the heavy burden of mythological imagery, now characterised by references to doom and disaster as opposed to the earlier heroic passion, joy and innocent pleasure.

In the peasant world the dominant imagery is of treasure, gleaming yellow gold, which substantiates the general motivation to material survival, on the one hand, and foreboding supernatural images such as human-headed owls as well as storms and other manifestations of nature on the other. In the same way the very language of the peasant characters is distinguished from that of their heroic counterparts and these contrasts reiterate and re-emphasise the basic dramatic conflict of the play. The peasants speak a stylised country dialect of Gaelic-English which was largely popularised by the Abbey Theatre and especially by the plays of Lady Gregory and John Millington Synge. It hardly matters whether that speech is an accurate and realistic transcription of actual dialects then in use. Its suitability and expressiveness are the real concerns. There is a good deal of non-English syntax and intonation carried over into Irish speech from Gaelic in any case which makes the language dramatically plausible. The concrete, homely vocabulary emphasises the debasing materialism which determines their lives. Individual speeches are short. The sentences are direct and declarative without much attempt at elegance or ornamentation. Although the dialogue is arranged into very carefully wrought verse, the abrupt and natural cadences of real peasant speech are suggested by using a flexible pentameter line which freely allows the addition of extra, unstressed syllables and is often mixed with equally flexible tetrameters.

> *Shemus.*   When the hen's gone,
> What can we do but live on sorrel and dock,
> And dandelion, till our mouths are green?
>
> *Mary.* God, that to this hour has found bit and sup,
> Will cater for us still.
>
> *Shemus.*   His kitchen's bare.
> There were five doors that I looked through this day
> And saw the dead and not a soul to wake them. (p. 13)

The heroic characters, on the other hand, speak a more formal and elevated language in which the basic poetic rhythms so carefully subordinated and camouflaged in the peasant speeches, are allowed to intensify and predominate. The verse becomes more regular, syntax and imagery more ornamental and archaic; especially in the lush speeches of the poet.

> *Aleel.*   A man, they say,
> Loved Maeve the Queen of all the invisible host,
> And died of his love nine centuries ago.
> And now when the moon's riding at the full,
> She leaves her dancers lonely and lies there
> Upon that level place, and for three days
> Stretches and sighs and wets her long pale cheeks. (p. 55)

Somewhere between the two extremes the other characters find a style of speaking suited to both their particular function in the drama and the consistency of lyrical effect which unifies the whole. In effect the language of the play imitates reality but with sufficient stylisation to distance the action from the reality of everyday life in order to suggest a deeper meaning behind it.

The stage setting which Yeats used for his own production was also highly stylised. Each interior was painted a single colour with glimpses of wood or garden through open doors and windows. The trees were painted in flat colours without light or shade against a gold or diapered background. The desired effect was that of a missal painting, alienating the audience from a sequence of action which purports to be realistic and governed by the traditional norm of logical plot progression.

THE LAND OF HEART'S DESIRE (1894)

Original Publication: London and Chicago, 1894
First Performance: London, 1894

The action of the play is no more realistic or believable than that of *The Countess Cathleen*, but it is certainly more straightforward in outline and more tightly constructed. The central figure, Mary Bruin, is seen at a point of momentous decision between the contradictions of the physical and supernatural worlds. The outcome is a foregone conclusion. Instead of the opposition between a peasant and heroic culture the action of *The Land of Heart's Desire* lies wholly within folk tradition. Unlike Cathleen, Mary is an introspective, emotional woman who is instinctively at odds with the kind of life she leads, whose imagination is fired by the tale she reads of Princess Edain in fairyland. Her progress towards self-fulfilment in the supernatural world is as direct as Cathleen's, but it is not complicated by either an antithetical figure such as Aleel or by the need for developed action. In order for the countess's natural concern for her fellow men to reach truly heroic proportions, a series of calamities were required. Famine, the theft of her treasure, the sale of all real property and the disappearance of the proceeds from that sale prepare the way for Cathleen's supreme sacrifice. Mary Bruin, on the other hand, is already at the point of decision and very little exposition or development is needed. Instead, we have an investigation of the various forces and pressures which affect that decision. Yeats concentrates on the interrelationship and strength of those forces as they are projected by the characters, the symmetrical structure of the action and the interplay of language throughout.

As the representative of imagination and intuition, Mary is set in opposition to the family into which she marries. Her mother and father-in-law are the contrary faces of age and materialism. Bridget is a sour, old woman, cross and jealous. Youth, beauty and the subjective life have no welcome in her scheme of things. Maurteen is a mellow, benevolent old man, who sets great store by the creature comforts and good life his worldly success has secured. He is fond of his son's pretty young wife and indulgent of her whims, believing that time will bring her to her senses and into conformity with the practical and narrow-minded women of his world. Shawn, the young groom, is kind and good like his father. His is the love of the physical body not of material goods, and his claim on Mary is a strong one, certainly not without its attraction for her. Father Hart, like the other men, is well disposed and understanding. He represents the love of god and life in the spirit from within an objective and practical, physical world which characterises Christianity. The reaction of the fairy child to the crucifix on the wall emphasises the preoccupation of Christianity with sin and suffering, with good conduct as an investment towards success in this world and salvation in the next. She, on the other hand, is the representative of an alternative world-view, a joyful, spontaneous existence untrammelled by time and change in which experience is its own reward. In making a decision, Mary is really choosing between the subjective freedom of fairyland and the objective self-denial of Christianity which includes within itself both the positive and negative qualities of all three Bruins. By particularising the various facets of material existence, Yeats provides the play with a realistic and balanced set of alternatives as well as the multiplicity of character relationships and interaction which drama requires. Mary, however, is as predisposed towards subjective freedom as the others are to appreciate the limitations and satisfactions of the human condition. Her withdrawal from the physical world and choice of a supernatural existence is attended by a sense of sadness and loss because of the sympathy the audience feels for the life she leaves behind.

The symmetry of the dramatic scheme also contributes to the effectiveness of the play and to its ritual quality. The entrance of the fairy child occurs at precisely the mid-point of the piece and the first half of the play concentrates on justifying the power exercised by the supernatural over the Bruin household in addition to establishing the relationships and representative values of the characters involved. Here Yeats relies on folk belief rather than legend and creates an original plot rather than following a known narrative model. The action is set in motion by the idea that supernatural agents are particularly active in the temporal world on May Eve and that to give them fire and milk on that day, however inadvertently, is to place oneself in their power. Without such documentation and Mary's wilful abandon in consummating her submission to the world of fairy, the subsequent action would be absurd. The power of the material world to hold Mary Bruin from her heart's desire is effectively cancelled, but the action is so carefully worked out that the audience is as slow as the characters to appreciate the fact. At first the fairy child seems to charm the older folk in a very natural way with her innocence, gentility and beauty. Even the cross-grained Bridget is won over to the point that she forgets her instinctive suspicion and offers the child fire to warm herself as well as milk and honey to replace the rejected bread and wine. The last vestige of safety or protection is removed when the child cries out in horror at sight of the crucifix and begs that it be taken away. So strong is her spell upon them all, that the old priest, assuming purity of intention and simplicity of mind, complies rather than upset her further. By the time her actual nature is revealed, they are quite powerless and cannot interfere with Mary's freedom of choice.

The imagery of the play, including the singing and dancing, and the patterned language of the dialogue are very important features of the composition. The characteristics of the two worlds are caught in the pagan images of magical quicken wood, fire and milk as opposed to the Christian crucifix, bread and wine, symbols of suffering and sacrifice. They are further contrasted in the lighthearted joy and ecstasy of fairyland as opposed to the monotonous toil and pain of mortal existence as well as in the opposition of eternal youth and inevitable old age. The quicken wood, a bough of mountain ash which Mary hangs upon the door post according to ancient custom to bring good luck to the household, is almost immediately stolen away by the fairy child in full sight of the audience. Just before the child's reappearance in the middle of the play, Mary recalls the images in her response to Shawn's attentions.

> O, you are the great door-post of this house,
> And I the branch of blessed quicken wood,
> And if I could I'd hang upon the post
> Till I had brought good luck into the house.
>
> (Yeats, 1966, pp. 192–3)

The image of Christ hanging upon the black cross, a symbol of yet another kind of love, quickly follows, implying that the love of material ease and sexuality is brought together in the binding love of god which in turn is sharply contrasted with the subjective anarchy and spontaneity of fairyland. The song, 'The wind blows out of the gates of the day' (pp.194–5, 200 and 210), which is repeated at the child's entrance, at the revelation of her true nature, and again at Mary's transition from one mode of existence to another, also functions as an image of that happy supernatural life. Its lyricism adds a new dimension to the action, as does the child's dance, and suggests the presence of an active supernatural agency better than any mere statement, however poetic. The repetition acts as a structural device and is closely linked to the echoing of ideas and even phrases from Mary's speeches during the first half of the play, in the fairy child's statements during the second half. In every aspect of its composition the unity of the work is insisted upon and within that unity contrasts and oppositions are emphasised.

The language and verse forms are very carefully worked out as expressive elements and subordinated to the symbolic action. Because there is no distinction between peasant and heroic dialects, the fabric of the verse is much more uniformly based on a fairly natural and unaffected blank verse which rises in lyrical intensity according to speaker and subject matter. The imagery and style are decidedly pre-Raphaelite in their reliance on stock imagery and archaisms. The dialogue is at its best when colloquial and concrete:

> *Shawn.* Do not blame me; I often lie awake
>   Thinking that all things trouble your bright head.
>   How beautiful it is – your broad pale forehead
>   Under a cloudy blossoming of hair!
>   Sit down beside me here – these are too old,
>   And have forgotten they were ever young. (p. 192)

In its final version (1923), Yeats distinguished between the play as a poem and as a theatrical text by enclosing purely lyrical or non-dramatic passages in brackets and advising players, especially amateurs, to omit them in performance. The work certainly gains in dramatic intensity by their omission. The metrical verse also gains in naturalness through Yeats's insistence that this action be distanced from our own time and conditions by means of costume and stage design, and that the movements of all actors other than those of the fairy child be reduced to a minimum.

CATHLEEN NI HOULIHAN (1902)

Original Publication: Dublin and London, 1902
First Performance: Dublin, 1902

Instead of a decision to escape temporal existence altogether, the hero of *Cathleen ni Houlihan* chooses between material comfort and self-sacrifice for the common good of his fellow men. Like the Countess Cathleen, Michael Gillane is in a primary phase of existence, he has an active and pragmatic personality. Rather than the heart seeking fulfilment in its own dream or imaginings, Michael is awakened to the possibilities of heroic sacrifice in terms of fulfilling his duty to his country and identifying with a world outside himself. The drama is conceived in terms of conflict between an ideal cause (national liberation) and private or personal good (marriage and material ease). The main character ultimately rejects his immediate self-gratification and assumes the stature of a tragic hero through his enlightened self-sacrifice.

The plot is very slight and there is little or no physical action except for the entrances and exits of the characters. Nor is there a precedent or model for the story. Yeats claimed that the idea had come to him in a dream, but the personification of Ireland as a troubled old woman seeking help has all the authority of actual folk belief which finds its origin in an animistic, pre-Christian tradition of supernatural intervention. An early version of the same symbolic figure is central to 'Hanrahan and Cathleen, the Daughter of Houlihan' published in *Stories of Red Hanrahan* (1897) and reprinted in *Mythologies* (1959). The exact nature of the ideal that Cathleen represents is very difficult however. What poetic images could one use to present an attractive and persuasive view of either a military rising or the national independence and cultural identity that would follow? Yeats wisely avoided the issue and rather than contrast the homely comfort of the Gillane household and their material well-being with some contradictory vision, the drama develops as a revelation or unravelling of Cathleen's mysterious presence.

The prosperity and good fortune of the Gillanes is established at once. Michael is marrying Delia Cahel, a beautiful, young girl with a handsome dowry. Fine new clothes have been bought, the wedding organised, and Michael's parents congratulate themselves on their success in life, especially since they began without the advantages or security they are now able to provide for their children. Peter and Bridget plan for the future; he to expand the farm, she to educate her younger son for the priesthood. The little boy looks forward to the greyhound pup his future sister-in-law has promised him. The entrance of the poor old woman is immediately arresting because of the obvious contrast she provides. Her curiously indirect replies and riddling statements make us strongly aware of some larger discrepancy between her appearance and reality. She is a stranger and complains that all do not receive her well, particularly the Gillanes' neighbour, Maurteen and his sons, who were busy shearing sheep. She confesses that she walks the roads, being troubled because her land has been taken from her. She begins to sing to herself mournfully, saying that the cheering they hear down in the town is the joyful sound her friends used to make when coming to visit her. She appears out of touch with reality, demented by her grief, and claims that many have died for love of her. Michael is obviously captivated by her tale and his mother wonders if she is from beyond the world. The old woman refuses money, which proves that indeed she is not of Bridget Gillane's world, and insists that any man who offers her help must give himself entirely to her cause. Michael offers to come with her to help her put the strangers out of her house, and his family, seeing the danger, try to call him back to the things of this world. The old woman sings again of the death and self-sacrifice her cause entails, but also of the fame and immortality that participation in it will bring. Enthralled, Michael turns his back on youth, material expectations, and even sexuality as the voice of the old woman again offers public recognition. He tears himself from Delia's arms to join the Irish patriots in the rising of 1798.

The significant action of the play is as much the gradual revelation of the old woman's metaphorical nature as it is Michael Gillane's decision to abandon his self-interest and fight for Irish nationalism. The old woman is not so much a real person as she is the representation of an ideal, the personification of an abstraction, and therefore a justifiable cause for Michael's irrational decision. He is mesmerised, enchanted if you will, by the metaphorical truth she expresses in her own person and in her plight as well as by the heroic attraction of fame and glory whether or not the rebellion succeeds. Michael is awakened to the possibility of heroic action through the ritualised presentation of the old woman's nature or character. The attention of the audience is so focused on the mystery she presents that Michael's lack of individuality is taken for granted. The play is a straightforward dramatic fable and it is the method as much as the meaning which holds our attention.

The careful exploitation of the old woman's almost supernatural presence and Michael's ready acceptance of its implications is theatrically effective. The stage properties and setting alone are sufficient to convince an audience of the physical well-being implied; the new clothes, the sack of money and especially the physical attributes of the young lovers. The cloaked figure and centuries-old face of Cathleen ni Houlihan belie her attractions and from that point on the action of the drama takes place as much in the imagination of the audience as it does on stage. Since her speeches cannot be taken as being literally true, the audience searches for the figurative meaning behind them. Michael, their representative on stage, registers their growing understanding and acceptance of that meaning. It is one of the strengths of the play that none of the characters acknowledges that meaning directly but that Michael is prepared to act upon it. Because attention has been riveted on the mystery of Cathleen's true identity and nature, the question of logical motivation for Michael's acceptance is avoided. Self-sacrifice is made to seem inevitable through the agency of supernatural intervention and the play is more properly defined as a dramatic ritual than a narrative.

The climactic moment is especially vivid and theatrical: Michael in Delia's arms, torn between his longing to cleave to her in contentment and the desire to follow the old woman into heroic glory. Cathleen's voice is heard from outside reiterating the promise of immortality and Michael physically breaks away. The unabashed sentimentality of the scene is transcended in the closing lines as the younger brother describes the transformed old woman: 'I saw a young girl, and she had the walk of a queen.' (Yeats, 1966, p. 231) The reality of Cathleen's transformation, which is also the proof of her supernatural nature, is reported verbally and left to the imagination of the audience while Michael's break with Delia is a concrete, theatrical image which is acted out on stage.

The same confrontation of verbal and dramatic imagery is emphasised by Cathleen's songs which carry the greatest burden of imagery antithetical to the Gillanes' material contentment: images of death and heroic glory. Her lyrics are far better integrated into the plot and certainly more expressive than those of Yeats's earlier plays. Mournful lamentation is native to the strange old woman and the lyrics constitute a carefully structured statement: 'I will go cry with the woman,/ For yellow-haired Donough is dead'; 'Do not make a great keening/ When the graves have been dug tomorrow'; 'They shall be remembered for ever,/ They shall be alive for ever'; and the final reprieve; 'They shall be speaking for ever,/ The people shall hear them for ever.' (pp. 223, 228, 229 and 231)

The style of the dialogue is a rather self-conscious prose which echoes country usage, especially in its slow and deliberate movement as well as in its abrupt and sometimes awkward syntax. The really striking feature of this language is the fact that its phrases are so nearly regular in length and stress pattern that they have the effect of verse even when furthest from it. At least the more passionate speeches can be read almost as verse.

> *Bridget.* Well, if I didn't bring much I didn't get much. What had you the day I married you but a flock of hens and you feeding them, and a few lambs and you driving them to the market at Ballina? [*She is vexed and bangs a jug on the dresser.*] If I brought no fortune I worked it out in my bones, laying down the baby, Michael that is standing there now, on a stook of straw, while I dug the potatoes, never asking big dresses or anything but to be working. (pp. 217–18)

In the mouth of the heroic Cathleen ni Houlihan the same effect is achieved.

Old Woman. It is a hard service they take that help me. Many that are red-cheeked now will be pale-cheeked; many that have been free to walk the hills and the bogs and the rushes will be sent to walk hard streets in far countries; many a good plan will be broken; many that have gathered money will not stay to spend it; many a child will be born and there will be no father at its christening to give it a name. They that have red cheeks will have pale cheeks for my sake, and for all that, they will think they are well paid. (p.229)

The simplicity and directness of both the vocabulary and sentence construction, along with the inversions and circumlocutions which derive from Gaelic, lend a musicality and quaintness which other country dialects of native English speakers could never achieve. The repeated grammatical constructions and balanced qualifying phrasing also echo the language of the King James Bible and heighten the effect, raising the language to the needed quality of poetic expressiveness. Altogether, it constitutes a successful vehicle both for subject matter and theme, especially in its progressive intensification to the level of verse and ultimately to the lyricism of intoned chanting or actual song.

THE POT OF BROTH (1904)

Original Publication: New York, 1903
First Performance: Dublin, 1902

Yeats's earliest plays are generally characterised by a degree of high seriousness, and the vision of human experience which he projects is one of heroic possibility and transcendence rather than of tragic flaw and downfall in the traditional sense. In *The Pot of Broth* we have a remarkable inversion of both subject matter and mode, a comic vision of life based on an anti-heroic conception which celebrates the same virtues that operate in the heroic or supernatural worlds of the earlier works. The play is one of the first of the dialect comedies written for the national theatre movement and however slight or trivial its subject matter, it was very popular as a curtain raiser, a short play performed before the main production for the purpose of rousing the audience. Such a piece might also be played between two more serious dramas in order to provide comic relief and a balanced view of the human condition through contrast. Comedy is, after all, the unmasking of absurdity, the presentation of inversion or inflation of experience in such a way as to encourage the audience to view it as amusing rather than frightening, reassuring rather than threatening.

Instead of a traditional hero, we have a tramp, a wanderer who has rejected conventional morality and values in favour of a more intimate relationship with nature and the wisdom of the peasantry. The tramp is more an archetype than a real person, and in this play, he has no name, nor is his personality well developed. Like his counterparts in Yeats's later plays, he is a joyful, spontaneous figure, a natural, free, and irrepressible force who delights in outwitting those who have fallen from their former innocence and unity of being into religious, economic, and social conventionality. The tramp is an anti-hero, the mask and mirror-image of the true hero, but a man who also transcends the limitations of modern life. In this particular case he proves the occult wisdom of Heraclitus: 'The way up and the way down are one and the same.' (in Wheelwright, 1959, p. 90)

The really interesting thing about the figure of the tramp in Yeats's plays and in the early Irish theatre in general, is that he is the prototype from which contemporary personifications of alienation and victimisation are derived. Tramps and tinkers were common in Ireland towards the end of the last century as they had been for generations, primarily as a result of political and economic repression. The penal laws, enacted in an effort to suppress nationalism and cultural identity as well as the older land distribution system which concentrated the largest share in the hands of the conquerors' Anglo-Irish descendants, caused continuing hardship and displacement of normal life. People took to the open roads both as refugees and rebels. Rather than exemplify the highest virtues and values of established society which were either tainted or perverted by British colonisation, the real folk hero, as celebrated in the nationalist theatre, was the rebel who rejected such ideals and resorted to a natural and anarchic mode of existence. His distinguishing characteristics were a sense of joy and spontaneity, the lyricism and spiritual responsiveness of the ancient Gael.

The tramp in *The Pot of Broth* lives by his wits. He is a conjurer, an artist of illusion, who gets his dinner by creating a web of words to ensnare the hard-bitten, closefisted Sibby Coneely. The plot turns on a point of common folk belief, the magic talisman given to a human being as either a forfeit or reward by a supernatural agent which produces all things for its owner. In folklore the motif usually figures in a story which demonstrates the deserts of the just and the punishment of the wicked, but Yeats uses the talisman as an instrument for the gentle exposure of avarice and pride. Knowing her character, the tramp appeals to Sibby's instinctive greed by offering her something rather than begging. He focuses her attention on the miraculous stone while he makes use of her provisions before her very eyes. Her avarice renders her gullible and her impatience urges the action along because the tramp must think up new and better tactics to divert her until the broth is actually cooked. Stirring the pot with a ham bone is a minor triumph. Insisting that the stone turns meat black if put in the broth on a Friday, as an excuse to drop in a whole chicken by way of demonstration, is brilliant. Even though the old religious stricture against eating meat on Fridays have been relaxed, the appeal to her religious prejudices and conventionality is obvious, especially as she begrudges the priest his dinner at her expense in the first place. The degree of comic exposure is again heightened as the tramp turns her mind from the stewing broth with personal flattery and appeals to her vanity. The domineering and almost shrewish wife is transformed into a simpering and defenceless creature by his tongue. Sibby begins to recollect herself, however, as the spell is broken by the tramp's abrupt preparations for a hasty departure and she gives little enough away. She offers nothing for the stone whose magical power she now accepts and seems to be settling down to a long, hard bargaining session. The imminent arrival of the priest who almost certainly will bring her fully to her senses, hastens the tramp's departure and he makes off with the meat and drink while keeping up his disarming patter.

The character relationships in this play are interesting in themselves, and especially so in that through them we begin to see a developing pattern in Yeats's conception of dramatic action. Here, we have a middle-aged or young woman who is placed between an old man whom she obviously dominates and a younger one who bests her at every turn. John is ineffectual (he nearly lets the old hen get away) and he is intimidated by Sibby (he drops the ham bone surreptitiously as she enters) while the tramp represents the anarchic and natural forces of rebellion. No description of him is offered, but he must be either young and vigorous or at least in the prime of life. The point is emphasised more strongly as John shows his respect and admiration for the younger man who gets the better of his strong-willed wife. Sibby's materialism is gently mocked in this little play and measured against the free-booting rebellion of the tramp. Similar kinds of opposition are also presented in the other early plays and generally expressed through a suggested sexual relationship: the Countess Cathleen deciding between Aleel and her Christian self-sacrifice, Mary Bruin between Shawn and the Fairy Child, Michael Gillane between Delia and Cathleen ni Houlihan and the comic inversion of Sibby Coneely between John and the tramp. In working out his parables and paradigms for the theatre Yeats continued to exploit this simple scheme of character relationships even in the later and more sophisticated plays.

The effectiveness of register and style also helps to account for the textural refinement and theatricality of *The Pot of Broth*. The speech rhythms of the country dialect are certainly faster and gayer than those of the earlier works, more imperative and emphatic. Yet the same kind of distinctive characterisation is attempted by heightening the regularity of sense units and relying on heavy inversion in order to give a greater sense of lyricism to the tramp's speeches.

> *Sibby.* Who is there? A beggarman,
>   is it? Then you may quit this house if you please.
>   We have nothing for you.

> *Tramp.*   It is a mistake you are making,
>   ma'am, it is not asking anything I am. It is giving I am more
>   used to. I was never in a house yet but there would be a
>   welcome for me in it again. (Yeats, 1966, p.241)

The tramp's gift for language seduces Sibby and provides the magical element within the aesthetic structure of the play which lends both the illusion and authority of reality to the action. The tramp's songs are also well integrated into the action and provide the intensity and transcendence of poetry so much a part of

Yeats's developing dramatic method. The first is an exultant cry of triumph at the thought of his plan to outwit Sibby, but the situation of the characters in the song is not unconnected with that of the play, 'There's broth in the pot for you, old man' (p. 239). The woman who voices the lyrics offers Jack the Journeyman beef, as opposed to broth for her old husband, and proclaims her preference for the sturdier male. The second song, 'My Paistin Finn is my sole desire' (pp. 247–8 and 9), is taken to be the lament of an unsuccessful suitor, but now the lyrics contrast with the stage action as we see Sibby's reason enthralled by the celebration of her charms and she is kept from retrieving her chicken from the pot.

There are a few references in the play to the heroic world of the Celtic past and to the supernatural, but these are not given particular prominence within the text. The images which are central to the action are physically present; the pot, ham bone, stone, and chicken, and they function at a purely literal level within the domestic scene. It may be that the objects also have esoteric or occult meanings as Yeats was much occupied with magical symbolism and Irish tradition at about that time. Images of the four treasures of Celtic mythology (the Dagda Mor's cauldron of plenty, the sword and spear of Lugh, and the Lia Fail or stone of destiny) appear in Yeats's poetry of this period and they correspond rather closely to the humble pot, ham bone and stone of the play. Of course, the comedy gives up its full meaning without reference to symbolic interpretation, but similar domestic imagery is also present in some of the later plays, where the contexts do insist on deeper symbolic meanings.

Besides the visible stage properties and the physical action of making the broth, the tramp's role is further emphasised by keeping the priest off-stage. There is an implied opposition between the two and a delightful irony in the tramp making off with the priest's dinner. The imminence of the priest's arrival also impels the action along from the very beginning. Without him the chicken would not have been dressed, and should he enter, logic and conventionality would be reasserted. The tension created is used to bring the action to a hasty and natural end while the ultimate exposure of Sibby's folly is left to the imagination of the audience. The actual appearance of the priest might deflect our interest from the triumph of anarchic freedom and the defeat of bourgeois materialism.

THE KING'S THRESHOLD (1904)

Original Publication: New York and London, 1904
First Performance: Dublin, 1903

The theme of *The King's Threshold* is the role of art in society, and its final revision presents us with both the tragedy of the poet's exclusion from affairs of state and the heroic death which proves him to be a man of action as well as one of ideals. The basic elements of the plot were taken from an obscure Irish legend and the hunger strike from Celtic tradition (it had not yet become a popular form of political protest). Yeats acknowledged his debt to Edwin Ellis's *Sancan the Bard* (1895) but his own version of the story shifts the basis of the conflict towards his personal preoccupations. The action of the play is conceived as a confrontation between the immortal aspirations of poets and the various forces of temporal degradation. The piece was originally intended as a farce, but the sober outcome insists on the essential seriousness of Yeats's view. The play celebrates the poet as an important legislator in human affairs. It is he who names all things and recognises their inherent qualities in the physical universe, who perceives and exposes correspondences between the temporal and ideal worlds. Without him societies inevitably descend to the trivial and ignoble.

The dramatic action which was conceived to express this simple theme is more particularly oriented towards satirising the defects and deficiencies of a society which no longer recognises the artist's role than in demonstrating that role directly. Seanchan does make a lyrical statement of the poet's true worth as his delirium approaches a moment of vision and Dyonysian ecstasy just before his death, but the greater part of the action is taken up by a series of representative figures who vainly tempt him to end his hunger strike, to accept the social inferiority and irrelevance of art. Seanchan represents the last poet of the bardic tradition and his heroic death is society's original sin, the fall from unity of being. Seanchan is both hero and poet, active and imaginative man, while only his pupils of all the stereotypes and caricatures who appear in the play, retain any semblance of imagination or intuition. They act as a kind of chorus and while the hero remains constant in his opposition to the king's wishes, they move from a stage of innocence to one of understanding and participation in their master's fate. Their values and judgment inform those of the audience by positive associations, just as those of the other characters repel by negative ones. The king, for example, who is the main antagonist represents reason, self-interest, and political expediency. He must subordinate the poet's wild freedom of imagination to his own will. He cannot give in to Seanchan. For the sake of law and order the poet must be excluded from the king's council at all costs. The king is the voice of corrupting materialism as we can see from the suggested bribe of land and treasure for Seanchan's submission. The other characters in the first of the two major confrontations are merely extensions of his nature, various manifestations of a demeaning and narrow self-interest which characterise society.

The mayor and cripples are the first to appear and they are even less individualised or developed as characters than the king and pupils. The baseness of their self-interest and stupidity is presented as farce and played off against the honest and straightforward folk wisdom of Brian, an old family retainer. The mayor's pretensions to power and authority of office are rendered absurd by his inability either to remember his speech or assess the situation intelligently. The pandering and scavenging of the cripples demonstrates the extreme result of deformed values among the town-dwellers. Nothing that these stick figures can say or do alters Seanchan's decision, nor will Brian's more realistic and moving exhortations. Even Brian's references to the pleas of Seanchan's father and especially his mother's understanding of the situation leaves him unshaken. Yeats rounds off the scene with a highly comic quarrel which ends in a Punch and Judy drubbing for the Mayor.

A more serious challenge is introduced as the chamberlain appears and restores order. With him are the representatives of those institutions through which social order is maintained, the army and the church. With neither understanding of nor sympathy for his position, both soldier and monk reject the idea of tempting Seanchan to eat. Instead they speak to him with condescension and disdain, but are properly put in their place by the dying poet's searing exposure of their hypocrisy. Chamberlain, soldier and monk, however, do not appear alone in this brief episode. The values they represent are strongly contrasted and also complemented by the character and actions of the court ladies whose entrance animates the scene. A definite pattern exists in which the poet is placed between opposed sets of

forces: king versus pupils; mayor and cripples versus Brian and
chamberlain; soldier and monk versus court ladies. With the
women, however, a different kind (or level) of temptation is
introduced. They are as frivolous and flighty as the mayor and
cripples are stupid and selfish. Their lives are dedicated to
pleasure, to singing and dancing. They wish Seanchan to break
his fast in order to provide them with music and song. Instead of
tempting him directly, they seduce the recalcitrant soldier to do it
for them. They hold his hands, stroke his arms, and gently
weaken his resistance to their will. From the failure of both army
and church to influence the poet's determination, the contention
of social authority is replaced by the temptation of sexual
attraction. The triviality of the court ladies gives way to the
seriousness of the two young princesses whose innocence and
beauty combine with their high station to suggest an ideal of
redemption or regeneration. Seanchan is not taken in by the
implied but hypocritical flattery. To be waited upon by the king's
daughters is not quite the same thing as being accorded
recognition as a counsellor to the king. Perceiving the
insidiousness of the king's intention, Seanchan exposes the
princesses as the innocent agents of corruption they are.

The final temptation is by far the most moving, the temptation
of a very personal and physical love for a real woman. As in the
case of the pupils and Brian, Fedelm is seen as a somewhat
realistic figure, perhaps more through the nature of her
relationship to Seanchan than through actual character
development, and the hero's reliance on her comforting support
in his delirium makes the point with admirable economy and
emphasis. Fedelm's love for Seanchan is very much of the
temporal world as opposed to that of the spiritual, but not
altogether possessive. Her ultimate argument for tempting him,
even attempting to trick him into breaking his hunger strike, is
that she can conceive of sharing him with another woman if it
comes to that, but not with death. It is an idea, like many others
in the early plays, which occurs again in later works; most
prominently in *The Only Jealousy of Emer*. Otherwise, the action of
The King's Threshold is more like that of Milton's *Samson Agonistes*,
and especially so in its calculated progression of temptations
which the hero surmounts as he moves closer and closer to a
revelatory death and apotheosis. From the pleading of Manoah,
Samson's father, through the commentary of the chorus, Delila's
attempts to regain his confidence and Harapha's challenge,

echoes persist, even though superfluous characters and action are included in *The King's Threshold.*

Yeats multiplies and overlaps the episodes in order to extend and balance the symbolic meaning. At the same time, he mixes serious argument against the poet's exclusion from the king's council with satire and sheer farce. Even the degree of stylisation in character development shifts from the representative and dehumanised figures of the king's party to the warmly human and sentimentalised followers of Seanchan. As King Guaire blusters back on stage to renew his opposition to the dying poet, we are more than ever aware of the fact that the play is rather contrived. The multiplicity of characters and actions arise from the need to captivate an uninterested audience and move them to sympathy with the theme through means other than the logical and inescapably meaningful symbolic scheme. The characters are given neither inherent nor arbitrarily assigned motives for their presence, and they have obviously been elaborated from four major types or figures: poet, king, pupils and lover. As it is, there is not much depth and significance to Seanchan's confrontation with society. As yet, Yeats had no audience for a starker and more stylised presentation nor even a thorough-going argument to prove that imagination should help to govern society. In this play the exclusion of a subjective poet from the king's council failed to capture the imagination of a popular audience while the inclusion of a wild and anarchic hero or warrior into the conventional and conformist council of another king proved more successful later on in *On Baile's Strand.*

The use of language is also a very important factor in any discussion of the play's relative merits. Styles of speech are employed as an effective means of characterisation and the major distinction is to be found in the degree of rhythmic invention and figurative ornamentation. From the pronounced lyricism of the poet and his pupils the dialogue shifts to the more formal, discursive and rather ponderous speeches of king and chamberlain.

Oldest Pupil.   I said the poets hung
   Images of the life that was in Eden
   About the child-bed of the world, that it,
   Looking upon those images, might bear
   Triumphant children, but why must I stand here,

Repeating an old lesson, while you starve?
                                    (Yeats, 1966, p. 264)

Chamberlain.   You wrong us, Seanchan.
    There is none here but holds you in respect;
    And if you'd only eat out of this dish,
    The King would show how much he honours you. (p.288)

Fedelm's speeches, as one might imagine, fall somewhere
between the two styles as befits the ambiguous attraction of her
love. A good deal of variety and not a little humour is also
achieved through the use of provincial dialects such as the rich
peasant speech of Brian and the emphatic prose of the mayor and
cripples. The contrasting social and ideological levels are
mirrored in the different registers of English while the
manipulation of rhythm is also used as a basic constructional
feature. The play begins in heightened lyricism but lapses into
looser prose which recovers itself in the quarrel between Brian
and the mayor where chanted curses in trimeters and tetrameters
have almost the effect of song. A similar effect is also achieved
through varying the line length of Seanchan's speeches and the
song he sings at Fedelm's entrance which signals the final crisis
and its resolution.

Verbal images and figures of speech are concentrated in those
passages which set out to achieve a lyrical effect, but for the most
part the physical elements of the stage picture are equally
important in expressing and emphasising the theme. Scattered
references are made to Celtic legends and heroes such as Finn,
Oscar and Grania as well as to the arcane pagan symbolism of sun
and moon (gold and silver) and the subjective, introspective
waterfowl, herons and cranes, so peculiar to Yeats's personal
philosophy. Even the Christian symbolism of the creation and the
Garden of Eden become almost obsessive in Seanchan's delirium
and the cripples introduce an obscure and almost irrelevant
reference to the holy well of a local Irish saint. Taken together,
they amount to a consistent preoccupation with the power of
creative imagination and art as an analogue of divine creation as
well as an archetype of ideal human conduct. The visible stage
pictures, on the other hand, tend to emphasise limited or limiting

conditions of physical or temporal existence. The cripples, for example, are physical manifestations of a debased and corrupt society which has lost sight of its ideals and imaginative archetypes. They are as deformed of body as the others are in mind or soul. They are paired against the imbecility of the mayor and together are contrasted with the beautiful court ladies whose only passion is for dancing and hurley. They in turn are paired with the unenlightened hypocrisy of chamberlain, monk and soldier. The whole action is played out before one of the most powerful images of all, the great door of the king's palace, while throughout the play, humble bread is visibly offered again and again to the poet who rejects life in a society which does not honour art. The young pupils and princesses can be said to represent an innocence and unity of culture which is about to be lost forever. The threatening halters worn by the pupils and the acquisition of leprosy levelled against the princesses are brought together in the paradoxical image of the moon which is normally a symbol of subjective and creative life, but in this case white with leprosy, an evil picture in the sky which is responsible for the contagion that afflicts mankind. Seanchan's triumph over his subjectivity is in embracing his antithetical nature, in experiencing the death of the hero as an objective man of action.

THE SHADOWY WATERS (1911)

Original Publication: London, 1900
First Performance: Dublin, 1904

There can be little doubt that *The Shadowy Waters* occupies a very important place among Yeats's plays, not only because of the evident concern he exercised in revising the original text, but also because the combination of elements and the structure into which they are woven achieve a more powerful effect than any of the earlier work and provide a basis for further development. The play dates back to the 1890s, but its effectiveness has little to do with the fact that the action is associated with a central myth of the ancient Celtic world. Rather than rely on the authority and nationalistic associations of mythic incidents and characters, Yeats recreates them as vehicles for his private philosophy and endows them with esoteric and idealised significance. In addition to the firm basis of a major myth and arcane meaning, *The Shadowy Waters* also has the benefit of an accessible and universalised love story.

According to Lady Gregory's account of 'The Birth of Cuchulain' in *Cuchulain of Muirthemne* (1902) which was one of Yeats's principal sources, Dectora, the sister of Conchubar and wife of Sualtim, was carried off on her wedding day by the god Lugh of the Long Hand. She returned rather mysteriously one year later with a son who later came to be known as Cuchulain, the hero of The Red Branch (Ulster) cycle of Celtic tales. Rather than re-emphasising the superhuman origins and nature of Cuchulain, the culture hero, as in the original myth, Yeats places a figure named Dectora in similar circumstances but she and her captor enter into a mystical marriage at the world's end. Dectora is stolen from King Iollan by the adventurer Forgael, a hero and artifex whose spells are cast by playing upon a magical harp. Forgael is obviously as much a poet and philosopher as he is a hero and man of action. The discontentment of his men and his lieutenant's loyalty assert his heroism and prowess in battle while his own speeches are given over to speculation on his quest for mystical experience beyond physical life. Forgael speaks directly of his search for immortality just as Dectora's ship is sighted. Here we can see that the philosophical or symbolic themes are directly translated into dramatic conflict between sharply defined and contrasted characters or motives. Forgael represents reason or mind seeking death and the life of the spirit beyond, while Dectora represents the human will in its search for the force and passion of physical life. The outcome of the play shows that in their union there is a merging or melting of opposites, a transmutation or mystical rebirth and resurrection. United, they represent perfect humanity, embracing both the desire of man and woman for one another as well as a desire for eternal and unified being. It is often pointed out that the characters are clearly autobiographical and that the play records the spiritual union which Yeats believed to exist between himself and Maud Gonne. There is some question, however, as to the relevance of such information and the degree to which it deepens our understanding of or response to the particular characteristics of the play.

The dramatic action is clearly as significant as the outcome. As soon as Dectora is taken, she attempts to command her captors using her authority as a queen. She tries to incite the sailors to mutiny and threatens suicide rather than sacrifice her pride and freedom to a commoner. Forgael, hero and artifex, controls the situation with his magical harp which acts as a sort of supernatural catalyst and subdues her will. Under a spell the sailors fall into a dream in which the murder of Iollan seems distanced from themselves and they are distracted by thoughts of the pleasure to be had from the skins of looted ale. Aibric, Forgael's lieutenant, takes up a ritual lament for Iollan, the dead husband and king, and Dectora joins the keening. The immediate event seems to her to recede into the mythic past and she recognises in Forgael her reborn or resurrected husband-king. The transformation is complete: the forceful and passionate human queen who very definitely casts an heroic shadow has grown larger than life and entered into a dream-like or ideal state through the identification of her being with that of Forgael. His nature, in turn, is completed and complemented by hers. He is sustained in his quest, and raised to her level through her love, just as she transcended immediate experience through the magical spell he played upon his harp.

The essentially symbolic action of *The Shadowy Waters* is central to Yeats's thought and the pattern recurs again and again in the later plays where a paradoxical or ambiguous attitude towards the action is also nearly always present.

> *Forgael.* But it was all deceit, and flattery
>   To win a woman in her own despite,
>   For love is war, and there is hatred in it.
>
> (Yeats, 1966, pp. 333–4)

Just as the perfected state of humanity is reached, Forgael recognises the ambiguity of his means and motivation. At the moment of his victory he laments the injustice he has done to Dectora's individuality, the subterfuge he has used against her. In the end, however, he allows himself to become reconciled by her love. The world drifts away, leaving them alone, 'awaiting death and what comes after, or some mysterious transformation of the flesh, an embodiment of every lover's dream.' (p. 340) More explicitly than any other work of the period *The Shadowy Waters* demonstrates Yeats's concept of tragic joy: 'for the nobleness of the arts is in the mingling of contraries, . . . perfection of personality [and] the perfection of its surrender.' (Yeats, 1961, p. 255)

The language which Yeats used for *The Shadowy Waters* is as consciously poetic as that in any other play of the period. The sailors speak a modified peasant dialect which is cast as prose, but its heightened imagery, inverted syntax and regularity of phrasing cause it to blend in perfectly with the more formal, yet modified, blank verse of the heroic characters.

> *First Sailor.* I will strike him first. No! for that music of his might put a beast's head upon my shoulders, or it may be two heads and they devouring one another. (Yeats, 1966, p. 330)

As one would expect, the use of this loose form of speech stops with the transmutation of Dectora's passion from a temporal to an ideal state. In fact, the turning point is further emphasised by the elevation of their speech to song. They leave the scene in search of pleasure, singing: 'Brown ale and yellow; yellow and brown ale; a goatskin of yellow.' (p. 337) On the other hand, the more formal patterning and richer ornamentation of the heroic speeches is strengthened by the use of common idioms and images, rendering the final version closer in texture to colloquial speech than any of the earlier plays.

> *Aibric.* The hold is full – boxes of precious spice,
> Ivory images with amethyst eyes,
> Dragons with eyes of ruby. The whole ship
> Flashes as if it were a net of herrings. (p. 337)

In such language contrasts we recognise the effort to reflect the merging of poetic construction with common or human passion. Yeats was also making a new departure from the unity of lyric effect (or tone) which he had so much admired in the essays of Walter Pater and the plays of Maurice Maeterlinck.

In general, however, the principal images which are used in *The Shadowy Waters* have a direct correspondence with a supernatural world. In many cases the metaphorical possibilities of the various images give rise to an allegorical reading of the play which re-emphasises the quest myth that is at its core. The human-headed birds which circle Forgael's ship are purified souls who will lead him to the west, a place of dream, vision, and mystical experience far away from everyday life. The sea is the material world and the boat, a human soul, which is guided by the morning and evening star (also the white fawn), leading men out of the darkness and passion of physical existence into some sort of spiritual regeneration. The golden net of chance or fate which brings Forgael and Dectora together and inescapably unites them, represents the inevitability of the universal pattern which reconciles all contraries. The crown of silver with which Dectora ennobles Forgael (subjective and creative man) signifies the distinctive nature of his union with ideal woman as opposed to that of his predecessor, golden-armed Iollan (objective and over-mastering man). In her dream-like state Dectora recalls her husband as being part of a mythic past and his death as though it had occurred one thousand years before. It can hardly be coincidental that Yeats's dialectical scheme of history is based on major cycles of two thousand years during which a primary characteristic exhausts or dissipates itself while an antithetical or contrary one develops from near nothingness to usurp its full power and place. The magical ritual which is being enacted is also strengthened by the repeated image of nine conquered nations, nine swords with handles of rhinoceros horn and nine spells of the magical harp. The harp is perhaps the most forceful of all the symbols used, not only because of its direct effect on the action but also in its actual physical presence on stage, especially as it bursts into flame when Dectora covers Forgael with her hair, signifying their sexual as well as spiritual union. Human hair, and especially female hair, had been a very important sexual symbol in literature from the time of the Pre-Raphaelites. The image of ideal love being expressed by a woman enveloping a man in her hair can hardly be misconstrued.

The visual import of the stage pictures and production method is also central to the achievement of *The Shadowy Waters*. In subsequent revisions the elaborate descriptions and exposition, esoteric symbolism, numbers of exits and entrances, and even realistic stage business were stripped away. Every possible effort was made in production to emphasise the ritual nature of the action rather than its immediacy as a human story. Just enough relationship to natural human passions was retained in the text to enlist audience sympathy and understanding, but the actual production under Yeats's direction emphasised remoteness from real life. The colour scheme was purposefully monotonous, with sets of dark blue and dark green, while Dectora's costume was a lighter green relieved by the faint glimmer of copper and, later, gold. The stage picture was obviously more decorative than actively dynamic and the lighting throughout was meant to suggest the even glow of not-very-bright moonlight. The voices of the actors were guided by the prosody of their lines while all physical actions were to be played with quiet gravity and rhythmic movement. Indeed, the effort to replace the heavy esoteric symbolism of earlier texts with a plain, passionate story was counterbalanced by the production method employed. As Yeats maintained in 1906, the audience was being asked to follow and understand the play as a fairy tale, which in many ways it is although there is also an unmistakable insistence on Yeats's perennial philosophy.

DEIRDRE (1907)

Original Publication: London, Dublin, and New York, 1907
First Performance: Dublin, 1906

In this play Yeats comes much closer to balancing surface realism and symbolic meaning than he had in *The Shadowy Waters*. The later attempt, however, tends to give as much weight to natural emotion and human psychology as to a representation of universal order or pattern. On the one hand, there is the heroic transcendence of Deirdre who masters the tragic situation in which she finds herself and meets her fate with renewed strength of character and noble decorum. On the other, there is the larger conflict of youth and age, of honour and passion, of public and private morality. Basically, the plot of *Deirdre* is exactly opposite to that of *The Shadowy Waters*. Instead of a spiritual regeneration through the union of a young adventurer with an ideal woman captured from an established warrior-king, we have the story of an older king who overcomes a young hero-lover and insists on the return of his betrothed. The stolen bride loves the younger man and prefers an heroic death to the king's bedchamber and state. Iollan was killed and replaced by Forgael, which strikes us as being right and natural, or at least psychologically satisfying in so far as the mythic pattern coincides with a normal human process. The young do, in fact, ultimately usurp the place and prerogatives of the older generation. It is wrong and unnatural, however, for Conchubar to reverse the order of things and betray Naoise in an attempt to unite himself with Deirdre. The terrible subversion of universal order is brought to a satisfying end by Deirdre's rectitude and heroic self-sacrifice. But in the process our attention is shifted away from the more abstract pre-occupations of the play and towards a concern with individual character development. The representative nature of the action is certainly emphasised but the personality and psychology of the heroine dominates our attention in the end.

The legend of Deirdre and Naoise is a very central one in Celtic mythology; it is a tragic love story of both cultural and individual significance. A number of versions exist and Yeats acknowledged that he found Lady Gregory's retelling of it to be among the best. That particular rendering was itself made up of elements taken from a large number of existing texts and merged together into a selection and emphasis of details. His conception of character, action, and meaning is unlike any other although in this play he follows the main outline of his source more closely than was his usual custom. In a characteristic way, Yeats plays the characters off against one another so that their relationships form a simple representative scheme or diagram of the passions and ideals which motivate them. Naoise and Deirdre, for example, are caught between Fergus and Conchubar. Both are old men and kings in their own right. Fergus is a man of honour following an earlier and ideal cultural tradition. It is he who has brought the lovers back to Ireland with sincere promises of Conchubar's forgiveness. The high king, on the other hand, is willing to compromise his honour in order to gratify his passions and represents newer and debased cultural dispensation. Finding himself in Conchubar's power, Naoise reacts as the ideal man of action he is. Both he and Fergus oppose the evil and injustice which confront them and prepare for heroic combat. Fergus goes off to raise the countryside while Naoise is outnumbered, captured, and killed. Age has used its power and prerogatives to prevent youth from usurping its place. The natural order of things is subverted and in that sense Naoise's death is a tragedy, but certainly not in the Aristotelian or classical usage of the word.

Deirdre, on the other hand, is as much a complex human being as an archetypal figure. Her heroic nature is shown to be in conflict with her human passion. The resolve to outface

Conchubar is weakened by her love for Naoise and fear for his safety. She pleads with the high king for his sake and even considers compromising herself in order to save her lover's life. But in the end her real values reassert themselves and she refuses to demean the ideal love which alone gives significance to her life. Deirdre's choice reasserts her transcendent and heroic stature. Like the protagonists of all the early plays she freely chooses her fate and ironically outmanoeuvres Conchubar by appealing to the sense of decorum and honour which he has already abandoned. He dare not have her searched for the knife, which he suspects she will turn upon herself. The shift from passionate pleading to cold detachment and mastery of the situation completes and perfects her character, elevating her to archetypal significance. Her death and reunion with Naoise is a paradigm of Yeats's tragic joy.

In addition to the philosophical patterning of his own convictions about universal order, Yeats also added three wandering musicians to the original legend and the effect of their interventions in the action is to divide the play into very definite episodes or scenes which are similar in conception to those of classical Greek tragedy. The musicians act as a chorus, supplying exposition and background information for the action as well as objective commentary on the situation and intimations of its outcome. Being mature women of some wider worldly experience, fortyish and handsome, they complement and even extend Deirdre's persona. They have heard of the preparations for a wedding feast at Conchubar's palace and instinctively distrust the suppression of the old king's natural jealousy. The women both introduce the action and offer lamentations at its close. They also intervene at two other points, neatly dividing the action into three subdivisions. In the first scene their forebodings are contrasted with the innocence and faith of Fergus and Naoise, in the second we have the revelation of Conchubar's treachery and in the third the spectacle of Deirdre coming to terms with her fate, both as a woman and a queen. A classical unity of time and place prevails throughout as in every play between this and *The Countess Cathleen*. The subsequent concentration on a passionate moment of experience is particularly effective in this instance because psychological as well as archetypal significance is insisted upon.

The songs which the chorus of musicians sing again demonstrate Yeats's control of lyric construction and integration. The first, "'why is it", Queen Edain said' (Yeats, 1966, pp. 352–3), opens the play and asserts the ambiguity of love, its sorrow and joy. The second 'Love is an immoderate thing' (p. 375), comes between the second and third scenes, re-emphasising the idea contained in the first and carrying the argument to its ultimate conclusion: 'love-longing is but drought/ For the things come after death.' On the other hand, the keening which follows Deirdre's death is like the dance of the fairy child in *The Land of Heart's Desire,* an effective theatrical device rather than a literary one.

The language of *Deirdre* is both poetic and unified. The earlier attempts to distinguish and contrast peasant and heroic registers give way in this play to a far more consistent and colloquial blank verse.

> *First Musician.*   I have heard he loved you
> As some old miser loves the dragon-stone
> He hides among the cobwebs near the roof. (p. 360)

The speeches of the heroic characters are not much different in effect, retaining a directness and naturalness which is well suited to the human and psychological character of the action.

> *Naoise.* What woman is there that a man can trust
> But at the moment when he kisses her
> At the first midnight. (p. 366)

Apart from the heightened lyricism of the songs, the only shift of style occurs during the passionate scene between Deirdre and Conchubar. As Deirdre pleads for her lover's life, her state of mind is suggested by breaking up the pentameter lines into shortened sense units whose coherence becomes more and more strained and frenzied as her emotion builds up.

> *Deirdre.* It was my fault. I only should be punished.
> The very moment these eyes fell on him,
> I told him; I held out my hands to him;
> How could he refuse? At first he would not –
> I am not lying – he remembered you. (p. 382)

After Naoise's death and her recovery of heroic stature, Deirdre returns to the neutral and natural rhythms of unbroken blank verse in which her calm determination and mastery of the situation are in striking contrast with her earlier distraught state.

Another of the achievements of this play is the success with which Yeats coordinates and integrates verbal and visual or stage imagery, emphasising and re-emphasising his themes. The mythological underpinnings of the plot, for example, are underlined by reference to 'The Wooing of Edain' in the musician's first song and another tale concerning Lugaidh Redstripe and a woman who was turned into a seagull for one half of every year. Edain, wooed by Midher, King of the Sidhe, had been reborn into this world as a fly through the machinations of her lover's wife, but Midher won her back to the other world in a game of chess. The fate of Lugaidh Redstripe and his seamew wife, according to the play, is also bound up with the game, for they had played chess on the night they died. The repeated reference to their fate is a foreshadowing of the outcome of the play. Visual as well as verbal imagery comes together in the physical presence of the chessboard which Yeats used in production to dominate one side of the stage and at which the hero and heroine sit to play. The connotations of a game which ritualises heroic combat are further exploited through the frequent reappearance of an exotic, dark-faced soldiery who support Conchubar in his personal opposition to traditional precepts of honourable conduct. It is these black pawns who capture Naoise and eliminate him from the game rather than allow him a warrior's honourable death in battle. He is taken ignominiously in a bird net and dragged on to the stage, a human spirit (bird) ensnared and overcome by a complex net of circumstances and actions (fate) for which he is partially responsible.

A second cluster of images is associated with the brazier of fire around which the musicians gather. They concentrate on magical and creative or life-giving forces as opposed to the chessboard and its associations with war, fate and death. In at least one of his productions Yeats allowed the fire to dominate the side of the stage opposite the chessboard, associating both speeches and actions with one principle or the other by placing the actor near them. The chorus of women is very closely linked to the ritual fire and at times even appears to be its priestesses. The flame motif is also found in the jewels with which Deirdre arms herself in preparation for her encounter with Conchubar and parallels the relationship between the chessboard and the hunting net as images of Naoise's archetypal significance. Deirdre adorns herself with fiery rubies taken from the dragon-glittering king of a far country and there is much talk among the women of dragons and philosopher's stones which suggest violence, magic, and the transmutation of base to pure values. Even the passage of time from Deirdre's flight with Naoise is given overtones of the magic number seven and she does, in fact, transmute or purify her baser human nature into an heroic ideal.

In addition to integrating visual with verbal images and investing stage properties with the force and significance of independent characters, Yeats also paid some attention to the design of stage sets which he wished to use as yet another expressive device. The rough room in which the action takes place is unremarkable in itself, but Yeats conceived of the landscape seen through the doors and windows as consisting of the great spaces of a wood and a leafy coppice at twilight, suggesting silence and loneliness. After experimenting with Gordon Craig's movable stage screens and the creation of atmosphere through lighting effects (1911), he suggested that perhaps the painted backdrop of wood and leaves, the darkening light of evening and glimpses of the barbarous dark-faced men, were perhaps not so successful as the same images projected as shadows by the blood-red light of the setting sun. The effect of such a scene and its development from the stylised background of a missal painting in *The Countess Cathleen* and harmonised colour symbolism of *The Shadowy Waters* is significant. In *Deirdre*, a considerable effort is being made to isolate the action and distance it from a context of flesh and blood realism while emphasising the presence of universal forces and patterns which animate the universe.

3 Experiments in Form and Theme

AT THE HAWK'S WELL (1917)

Original Publication: New York, London, and Dundrum, 1917
First Performance: London, 1916

It is often said that *At the Hawk's Well* is a ritual of initiation and that is true to a large extent, but it is difficult to say exactly what Cuchulain is being initiated into since he shows no real awareness or understanding of what his confrontation with the guardian of the well might mean. Although the protagonist is the central figure in the Celtic cycle of the Red Branch of Ulster, the action of this particular play is taken from outside that body of material. Its meaning as well as conception and overtones are indeed alien to Irish legend. For Yeats Cuchulain represented the archetypal hero and completed individual who contained in his own person the objectivity of the man of physical action with the subjectivity of the man of imagination and intuition. In general Cuchulain characterises the unity of culture as well as of being, in the cycle or age which preceded the Christian era and provided its opposite or mask. The series of five plays which chronicle the significant turning points in Cuchulain's life and assert his symbolic significance begins with *At The Hawk's Well* although that was not the first to be written. In it we see the transformation of a reckless and over-reaching youth into a hero who enters upon his life's pursuit, his true role.

The story as Yeats conceived it is a very simple one. Cuchulain is an impulsive young man, entirely without self-doubt, who has set out to make an assault upon godhead or spirituality, to wrest for himself the waters of immortality and creativity. Obviously, this is not a subjective grail quest with all the trappings of spiritual allegory and Christian symbolism. Instead of regret for his failure, the hero leaves the stage exultant in his new purpose, the pursuit of a natural goal in an encounter with the woman warrior, Aoife. If not Cuchulain himself, at least the audience is aware of his transformation through a confrontation with the guardian of the well who is the representative of supernatural power, being possessed by the woman of the sidhe (the ideal woman as manifested in the supernatural world) at the moment when the miraculous waters flow. The goddess-guardian lures Cuchulain from the spot and seduces him into the woods where she hides herself from him. His desire for intercourse with the supernatural is unconsummated. Without regret he turns to pursue conquest and physical love in the world of nature and so asserts his objective character as well as that of his age.

The plot as outlined above is little more than an episode and the dramatic conflict at its centre is re-emphasised by multiplying relationships. Cuchulain (objective hero) not only confronts the woman of the sidhe (subjective ideal) but as an active and instinctual young man, he is set in opposition to the passive old man who has waited by the well for fifty years, warming himself by the meagre fire he is barely able to maintain, dry stick by dry stick. Most of the actual dialogue is between the old and young men who represent opposing modes of human conduct, opposite methods of controlling human experience. The subjective efforts of age give way before the dynamic objectivity of youth but in the end the young hero is outmatched by the power and menace of the supernatural world. Cuchulain's objective nature is completed, however, when he turns his attention towards the human and objective counterpart of the subjective spiritual ideal, towards Aoife and her warrior band. For a moment the inevitable oppositions which constitute the universe have intersected and by their careful arrangement and weighting, they have been reconciled: flesh and spirit, youth and age, male and female, war and love. Cuchulain's initiation is complete, but his ultimate degradation is also suggested through the curse of the sidhe which is reported by the old man. Cuchulain's initiation is thus ambiguous in that it inevitably contains the seeds of his fall from unity of being through the mixing of hatred with love and the slaughter of his only son, the boy born to Aoife.

In addition to the multiplicity of characters and action which is gained by introducing the old man into the plot, the use of the chorus in *At the Hawk's Well* is singularly effective. As in *Deirdre*, where the chorus provides an introduction to the action and marks its interior sub-divisions by offering commentary and direct dialogue, the chorus of *At the Hawk's Well* is a necessary part of the action. Instead of having a realistic and rational relationship to the main characters, the chorus exists outside the dramatic action and acts as an intermediary between it and the audience. The musicians introduce the action with the song, 'I call to the eye of the mind' (Yeats, 1966, pp. 399–400), which provides all the exposition necessary to an understanding of the play. Later, they intervene in the action at its climactic moment when the guardian is possessed and seduces Cuchulain from his avowed purpose. At the end of the play, after the hero's final exit, they again return to the stage and close the action with an unreserved affirmation of physical or temporal existence in the song, 'Come to me, human faces.' (pp. 412–13) As always, they speak from a position of omniscience, providing information and understanding which could not be easily expressed by the protagonists. The chorus orchestrates our response to the action. They create a mysterious atmosphere with their unnatural knowledge, weird appearance, ritual movements, musical accompaniment and lyric chanting. The effect they produce is to distance the action from the world of the audience and encapsulate it in a highly stylised, self-conscious world of art. The conception is highly theatrical, especially in the choral intervention at the moment of climax after a long dialogue between the protagonists. The illusionism of the scene which has come into being by stages is broken by the singing of several voices which serves to emphasise the intervention of the supernatural through the guardian's dance. The presence of the chorus reminds the audience that it is participating in an imaginative rather than a so-called real action with the result that attention is directed towards its possible meanings.

Yet another level of interaction between opposites exists in the contrast between the verse form associated with the musicians and that used by the heroic characters. Both old and young man use a rather formal and slightly archaic style whose word choice and phrasing is consistent throughout and shows them to be complementary figures. The speeches are cast in iambic pentameters and have a notably emphatic and heroic ring to them as well as a certain naturalness which results from enjambment and variation of the basic verse form.

Old Man. I have snared the birds for food and eaten grass
    And drunk the rain, and neither in dark nor shine
    Wandered too far away to have heard the plash,
    And yet the dancers have deceived me. Thrice
    I have awakened from a sudden sleep
    To find the stones were wet.

Young Man.   My luck is strong,
    It will not leave me waiting, nor will they
    That dance among the stones put me asleep;
    If I grow drowsy I can pierce my foot. (p. 406)

The line, 'I have awakened from a sudden sleep' is a subtle variation in rhythm and length on those which precede it. At the same time unusual phrases such as 'It will not leave me waiting' and 'they that dance among the stones put . . . ' raise the speeches beyond the merely colloquial and the action beyond that of every-day life.

The language and verse rhythms of the musicians provide a marked contrast with those of the main characters.

When I wrote in blank verse I was dissatisfied; my vaguely mediaeval *Countess Cathleen* fitted the measure, but our Heroic Age went better, or so I fancied, in the ballad metre of *The Green Helmet*. There was something in what I felt about Deirdre, about Cuchulain, that rejected the Renaissance and its characteristic metres, and this was a principal reason why I created in dance plays the form that varies blank verse with lyric metres. (Yeats, 1961, pp. 523–4)

Whether sung or spoken, the lines delivered by the musicians have a much greater lyrical intensity than those of the protagonists and that intensity is imparted by a shortened poetic line and one free from both inversions and archaisms. The more complex grammar of the longer pentameters is replaced by a simpler and stronger phrasing.

Young Man. Run where you will,
    Grey bird, you shall be perched upon my wrist.
    Some were called queens and yet have been perched there.

First Musician [speaking]. I have heard water plash;
　　it comes, it comes;
　Look where it glitters. He has heard the plash;
　Look, he has turned his head.

Musicians [singing]. He has lost what may not be found
　Till men heap his burial-mound
　And all the history end. (Yeats, 1966, p. 410)

The innovation is certainly successful and in addition to traditional characterisation through speech styles, Yeats has underscored the symbolic pattern of the action and of its emotional dynamics.

The imagery of the play is obviously centred on the hawk and well of the title but their significance and field of association for Yeats is not immediately clear from the text alone. The hawk is one of the many incarnations or manifestations of a spiritual ideal which Yeats associated with an eternal and perfect female figure. Because of the attraction and opposition between the spiritual and temporal worlds, this figure represents both love and war as we can see by her seduction of Cuchulain and the rousing of her human counterpart, Aoife, against him. On the great wheel of *A Vision* the spiritual ideal is incarnated as an aggressive and predatory hawk at the beginning of a cycle which is characterised by complete objectivity. The hawk's immediate association with the well may come from the legend of Niall and his brothers in which the hero makes love to the haggish guardian of a well (see Jeffares, 1970, p. 88), but in the context of the play the well is also justified as a point of contact between the two worlds. The supernatural waters of inspiration and regeneration are common enough in world myths, legends, and folklore. Yeats was well acquainted with several different versions: the magic well of Connla, the druid who was its guardian, for example, or literary works such as William Morris's *The Well at the World's End* (1896) and the Japanese nōh, *Yōrō* (The Sustenance of Age) by Zeami Motokiyō (1363–1443). In the Japanese play, local peasants, a father and son, are questioned by a court official about the miraculous waters of a fountain of youth whose fame he has been sent to investigate. They finally reveal their divine natures and dance out a benediction upon the land and the emperor's reign.

In Yeats's play the miraculous flood is very naturally awaited in a barren landscape, rockbound and windswept, at the foot of dry and leafless trees and in the presence of a withered old man. Only through water and love can life be generated while violence and hatred, as in Cuchulain's later relationship with Aoife, destroy it.

The use of imagery, however, is not limited to mere literary or verbal figures; the well is physically represented by a stylised square of blue cloth on the floor, and the hawk costume of the guardian as well as the image on the cloth folded by the musicians at the opening and closing ceremonies are effective theatrical or visual images whose meaning is strongly reinforced by association and contrast with the verbal figures. More important still as an extraliterary device is the guardian's dance which provides the climactic moment of the drama and suggests rather than defines meaning. In the same way that the dance of the fairy child in *The Land of Heart's Desire* characterises the nature of supernatural existence, the guardian's dance is a visible analogue of the creative power, violent antagonism and sexual attraction which characterises the relationship Yeats believed to exist between the supernatural and natural worlds. Both the dance itself and the visible images of well and hawk are expressive elements which maintain a necessary distance from every-day reality and force attention on the meaning of the strange events taking place on-stage. Yeats wished to make the theatre a place of intellectual excitement in which plays should serve the cause of beauty and truth by orchestrating and subordinating production methods to a total effect. He wanted a fusion of language, stage picture, music, and gesture in which scenery and costume were a background, in which music and gesture were an accompaniment to speech, not its rival. *At the Hawk's Well* was the first of the dance plays which in turn constituted an innovation in dramatic form. It relied heavily on production method for its effect and attempted to express an abstract concept directly through theatrical images and symbolic actions which have little to do with every-day life. In the dance plays Yeats finally escaped from traditional ideas of theatre. His introduction to Ernest Fenollosa's translations from the Japanese nōh had helped to crystallise his ideas and the fruits of earlier experiments into an exciting new concept. Highly ritualised actions replace narrative plot progressions and only the turning point or climax of a situation is shown. Instead of realism, the action is recreated in the imagination of the audience by presenting it as though an epic or bardic recitation were being acted out. The story is not so much told, as it is remembered and relived with attention focused on its representational (non-illusionistic) character. Instead of a conventional stage and controlled lighting, any bare space before a wall or screen with the ordinary light of a normal room is used. The audience is made to confront symbolic characters and actions directly. An atmosphere of ritual is established by the folding and unfolding of a patterned cloth, by musical accompaniment and chanted or sung lyrics. The figures in the play are either masked or have their faces made up like masks, and they move in a stiff hieratic way. There is no scenery, but highly stylised costumes and stage properties complete the presentation of an art world outside every-day life which yet reflects or projects some vital truth about life. *At the Hawk's Well* is a singular accomplishment in the history of theatre and a major statement of Yeats's most characteristic themes. It certainly warrants more consideration than would at first appear from its brief text and seemingly inconclusive action.

THE GREEN HELMET (1910)

Original Publication: Dundrum, 1910
    as THE GOLDEN HELMET: New York and Stratford-upon-Avon, 1908
First Performance: Dublin, 1908

Written more than seven years before *At the Hawk's Well*, *The Green Helmet* offers us a picture of the magnanimity, joy, and spontaneity of a truly heroic personality as it is tested in situations which derive from actual Irish myths. The play was written as a curtain raiser for the tragic action of *On Baile's Strand* (1904). Its comedy was meant to serve as a contrast to the high seriousness of the still earlier play and to complete a larger vision of man's total experience of life such as that found in the classical Greek or Japanese theatres which combine comic and tragic plays in a single day's performance. Following *At the Hawk's Well,* the action of the play presents the joyful apotheosis of the hero and demonstrates the regenerative power of his self-sacrifice and disinterested courage. It is an exact counterpart or anti-self to the plot of *Deirdre* and restores an essential nobility – harmony and honour – to Irish culture. The correspondence between the pettiness of heroic Ireland as it is satirised in the play, and that of Yeats's own time, which is characterised by the hypocritical hue and cry over J. M. Synge's *The Playboy of the Western World* (1907) [reprinted in *Collected Works*, 1962], should not be altogether overlooked.

> Here neighbour wars on neighbour, and why there [sic] is
> no man knows.
> And if a man is lucky all wish his luck away,
> and take his good name from him between a day and a day.
> (Yeats, 1966, p.423)

The open-handed heroism of Cuchulain in *The Green Helmet* is exactly the ideal of conduct Yeats wished to restore to modern Ireland.

The Green Helmet differs in construction from the plays that precede it. Instead of a single action, there are three separate episodes, each with its own resolution, which are linked together by character and theme. The quarrel among the three warriors as to which of them should wear the green helmet, symbol of superiority, is settled by Cuchulain's magnanimity and mature judgement. They fill the helmet with ale and share it equally. The war of words of the women of Ulster is also resolved by Cuchulain who bars Emer from entering until Laegaire and Conall have broken holes in the wall so that the three wives may enter the hall on the same instant. In the third episode he freely offers his own life as a pledge for the honour of his people and their traditions. In each case, however, the attempted resolution of conflict is subverted by the red man, Cuchulain's real antagonist, who represents an elemental or supernatural force in the universe which is the antiself or mask of heroic man. The action is very tightly constructed and opens with the challenge to a beheading contest. In order to stir up strife among the heroes, the helmet trick is introduced and they are challenged to decide which of them should have the honour of wearing it. Even the stable boys take up the quarrel but Cuchulain's good sense prevails. They are then interrupted by their wives who have been set to fighting over whose husband should be acknowledged first among the heroes. The women and servants fight on, well beyond their simultaneous entrance into the hall, and in spite of the fact that Cuchulain throws the helmet into the sea in order to put an end to such discord and contention. They are only silenced by the red man himself, who comes to claim Cuchulain's life. When the hero's head is proffered unhesitatingly, the red man gives him and him alone, the helmet, for he has thus proved his primacy over all the heroes of the land. The play proclaims Cuchulain an archetypal hero, and his contention with Laegaire and Conall over the green helmet is a dramatic invention which exists to measure that supremacy. In the same way, Emer is specifically recognised as the archetypal heroine, ideal woman, and perfect complement to Cuchulain while the red man is their supernatural counterpart, or at least that of Cuchulain. He interferes in the temporal world in order to establish its ideal image. The scheme is not very different from that of *At the Hawk's Well* except for the episodic nature of its construction.

The relationship between the characters and actions of the play and those in the original Celtic legends is quite another matter, however. The Cuchulain of *The Green Helmet* is a rather improbable character when measured by the standard of heroic conduct in 'The Feast of Bricriu' or 'The Championship of Ulster'. Even according to Lady Gregory's patchwork version, the legendary Cuchulain is not behindhand in fighting Laegaire and Conall to assert his superiority over them. While the others break holes in the wooden planking to make doors for their wives, Cuchulain heaves up the whole side of the great hall, allowing one hundred and fifty women to enter with his own wife at the same moment. The supposition that the ideal man of action is magnanimous and just is altogether foreign to pre-Christian Ireland and Yeats's characterisation in the play is as uniquely his own creation as Forgael's subjective quest for union with the supernatural in *The Shadowy Waters* or Cuchulain's objective assault upon it in *At the Hawk's Well*. Apart from the super-imposition of his own values and world-view Yeats has merely compressed the action of the heroic tales and by doing so has given it a good deal more emphasis and dramatic unity. In the original, Bricriu, a kind of trickster figure or manifestation of discord, calls a feast in order to sow dissension. Three distinct series of tests are undertaken in order to determine the championship of Ulster and three separate individuals act as judges of the context. As the tests progress in difficulty, the heroes confront the supernatural world directly and the final trial is the mysterious giant's solemn pledge to behead the man who beheads him. Yeats condensed and reorganised the action, combining the figure of Bricriu with the giant and motivating the whole by means of an opposition even more fundamental and widely accepted than that of the Celtic principle of order and discord. The red man is also a trickster figure but the conflict he introduces into this fictional world ends in the restoration of honour and harmony in society. His nature is suggested by the red he wears and his relationship to Cuchulain by the green of the helmet which characterises ideal heroism. In 'The Championship of Ulster' the token which confirms the right to the hero's portion is a golden drinking vessel, but Yeats turns it into a green helmet which at one point is filled with ale; the red and green are complementary in one sense and antagonistic in another. The red of fire and the sun which both destroys and regenerates; the green of living nature which dies and is reborn. A red man and green man were vital symbols in early fertility cults and both have survived into the Christian era in the figures of the devil who lives in a fiery hell, and the god whose death and resurrection is celebrated annually in Spring. By invoking the most basic ritual conflict and resolution known to the peoples of Europe and Asia minor, Yeats attempts to link the Celtic past with modern Ireland and to justify his conception of human personality, history and universal (supernatural) order. Cuchulain's spontaneity, sense of honour and disinterested courage is acknowledged by the supernatural world in the figure of the red man and an ideal image of social conduct is created, one which relies upon laughter and gaiety.

There is, of course, a good deal of comedy in the actual situations; the posing and boasting of the characters as well as the bawling and brawling of the climactic scene, but the sense of vitality and joy which characterises the play comes from the language itself. Yeats acknowledged his debt to the alexandrines of Wilfred Scrawen Blunt's *Fand* (1907) and referred to the verse form as a ballad metre, but hexametres are not all that common among traditional ballad forms while the freedom taken with unaccented syllables and internal breath pauses (caesurae) gives a far less formal effect than exists in either source. The genius of Yeats's conception is the use of blank verse with enough extra unstressed syllables to give a rippling, tripping, swinging rhythm to the lines.

Laegaire. What is that? I had thought that I saw, though
        but in the wink of an eye,
    A cat-headed man out of Connacht go pacing and spitting
        by;
    But that could not be.

Conall. You have dreamed it – there's nothing out there.
    I killed them all before daybreak – I hoked them out
        of their lair;
    I cut off a hundred heads with a single stroke of
        my sword,
    And then I danced on their graves and carried away
        their hoard. (p. 422)

Variations in the line through the repetition and contrast of words
or phrases not only permit emphasis and naturalness of speech
but also allow for the close control of lyric (musical) and even
emotional effects.

Cuchulain. Old Herring – You whip off heads! Why, then,
    Whip off your own, for it seems you can clap it on again.
    Or else go down in the sea, go down in the sea, I say,
    Find that old juggler Manannon and whip his head away.
                                                    (p. 434)

The return to a light and rolling triple metre is inevitable in that
speech as elsewhere in the play and re-establishes the
characteristic gaiety of the piece.

    The most drastic deviation from this ground rhythm is found in
the two songs which are written in very short and emphatic line
lengths. The swaggering and boastful lyric, 'Laegaire is best'
(p. 436), is made up of very regularly and heavily accented
dimetres while Emer's 'Nothing that he has done' (pp. 446–7 and
449) is modulated by occasional trimeters which add to its more
passionate lyricism. Both contrast sharply with the far greater
length of the basic verse form and each is effective in reinforcing
the dramatic tension of the scenes, especially Emer's, which is
accompanied by music and holds the stage until the three wives
sweep into the hall at the same moment. For further emphasis
Emer soon sings the song again and it is followed by the riotous

climax of the scene. The third episode or action in the play has no musical intervention but is sufficiently underscored by the concentration of verbal and visual imagery. Where the first song parallels the opening action and the second contrasts with its tumultuous context, the third scene, which is set off from the previous action by a blackout, is dominated by supernatural intervention and climaxed by the proffering of the helmet rather than the expected sword stroke.

The imagery of the play is very closely coordinated and visual images predominate. At that particular stage in his development Yeats was experimenting with pronounced colour schemes and strong decorative effects which might unify and reinforce the action as well as distance it from every-day reality and call attention to its meaning or relevance. The setting is meant to be orange-red and black with tinges of purple while the characters of the heroic world are dressed in various shades of green. Through the open door and windows green is repeated in the shining of the (subjective) sea, while the supernatural figures antagonistic to Cuchulain are dressed in red or black. The visual import is very strong, and meaningful relationships or associations are underlined by the colour scheme. The dark soldiery with eared caps derive from the cat-headed monsters of 'The Championship of Ulster' and are also, perhaps, related to the dark and exotic warriors of *Deirdre*. Black cat-men are very congenial images for Yeats and the perfect counterpart for the red man who is the objective force of fire or the sun in the supernatural world, because of their immediate association with subjective night and the moon.

Less powerful, but none the less striking, are the images of severed head and green helmet. At the beginning of the play Conall tells of the cutting off of the red man's head which went on laughing at him where it fell upon the ground until it was picked up by its owner who disappeared with it into the regenerating water of the sea. The image of dead men laughing, of severed heads which sing, is a frequent symbol of the proper relationship between the natural and supernatural worlds in Yeats's work, while the warrior's helmet, here a symbol of regeneration through spontaneous and selfless courage, is never used again. The device, however, does contain the ambiguity of those related images which Yeats used to express similar concepts. Cuchulain throws the helmet into the sea in order to end the discord which has brought chaos to the scene, but the red man brings it back and crowns him with it as a symbol of his archetypal nature rather than strike off his head with the two-handled sword he also carries.

In each case the encounters are further defined and characterised by actual stage pictures or theatrical images; the green helmet as a representation of contention and reconciliation, the entrance of the wives in a burst of song and tumult, and the appearance of a threatening devil-figure and cat-headed men of the supernatural world. Even without the presence of anti-illusionistic or distancing devices *The Green Helmet* is a tightly constructed piece of theatre, its character relationships, episodic construction, rhythmic movement, stage business, and imagery all contribute to the immediate and complete communication of meaning.

ON BAILE'S STRAND (1904)

Original Publication: Dundrum, New York, and London, 1903
First Performance: Dublin, 1904

Yeats took a good deal of trouble over this play and rather than a single, intense action or a series of parallel episodes, he conceived of its action as a layered pattern, the heart of which is Cuchulain's acceptance of Conchubar's oath and the consequences which followed. The same Cuchulain who would tame the hawk woman of the air (*At the Hawk's Well*) and proved himself worthy of the hero's crown (*The Green Helmet*) is now tamed in his turn, his wild anarchy subdued by the pressures of materialism and social convention. The tragedy here, in the popular sense of the word, is the hero's inclusion in the selfish and petty degradation of Conchubar's court, rather than the poet's exclusion from the council of state (*The King's Threshold*). Only the second half of the action concerns itself with the consequences of taking the oath, while in the first we find a suggested rationale for Cuchulain's submission. Conchubar requires the oath to ensure the succession of his sons and to placate his nobles who both fear and envy Cuchulain's heroic license. Cuchulain rails against the king's fall from the high heroism of their youth, but Conchubar will not be put off and insists on conformity with the changing temper of the time. He taxes Cuchulain with having no son to protect, for whom to secure the future. The hero's assertion that he is content to leave a name on a harp rings hollow. He then recalls the ecstasy of his youthful relationship with Aoife, bitter antagonist in battle and responsive lover. A comparison of that heroic occasion with the present lapse from unity of being, silently convinces him that he may as well take the oath of submission. Cuchulain realises that he has outlived his own age and believes that he has failed to reproduce its image, or at least acknowledges that assumption in giving way to immediate pressures and submitting to Conchubar's oath.

The second half of the main action is the real point of the play. Cuchulain is driven, unknowingly, to challenge his only son and overcomes him, as one might expect, thus destroying his own heroic image and putting an end to his line and *ethos* forever. Both a fall from unity of being and unity of culture is implied in the action and because of the oath, Cuchulain has no choice but to follow Conchubar's command. Much of the dialogue is taken up with establishing the presence of a natural blood-bond between the hero and his son. Cuchulain does not know who the boy is, but instinctively wishes to protect and befriend him. This feeling is so strong that he raises his hand against the high king, contrary to the oath he has just sworn. The other kings cry out that witches are responsible for this unthinkable act, but the audience knows better. Conchubar exercises his authority over Cuchulain, forcing the disastrous fight between him and the boy.

Conchubar's responsibility for the outcome of the action is central to Yeats's dramatic conception and constitutes a noticeable departure from the sources he used. In Lady Gregory's version of 'The Only Son of Aoife' Cuchulain acts on his own authority and in conformity with heroic tradition, but Cuchulain is a very young man according to the legend, while Yeats causes him to age along with himself and so introduces a self-conscious biographical element in the characterisation. Cuchulain's nostalgia for a fleeting affair in youth and his longing for a son, certainly has more to do with Yeats's imagination than with Celtic mythology. The more authoritative and up-to-date translation of the tale by Thomas Kinsella gives us a Cuchulain who acts solely from an ideal of a hero's honour, knowing all along that the challenger is his only son. According to that version, it is Cuchulain himself, and not Aoife, who makes the condition at the boy's birth that he reveal his name to no man, make way for no man, and refuse combat to no one. In Yeats's play Cuchulain shares responsibility for the disaster with Conchubar. Rather than follow the logic of natural affinity for the boy, Cuchulain is false to himself and the tradition of heroic honour which he represents when he obeys Conchubar. Of course, it would be equally dishonourable to break the oath, but the fundamental error lies in giving way to despair and submitting to the oath in the first place. Cuchulain and Conchubar are really complementary figures: a man and mask or self and antiself. If we take Cuchulain to represent action and intuition, Conchubar is easily recognised as a man of circumspection and reason. When one gives way to the other, an imbalance results; the perfect tension and equilibrium towards which the universe strives in order to complete itself is destroyed. Such a scheme of symbolic types was not a new departure for Yeats; the wise man and fool of *The Hour-Glass* preceded the present image and a number of similar examples followed; Cuchulain and Bricriu (the red man) in *The Green Helmet* as well as in *The Only Jealousy of Emer* and the young man and old man of *At the Hawk's Well*. In the first play of the Cuchulain cycle, the spontaneous man of action prevails, and he confirms the character of the objective or heroic age. In the action of *On Baile's Strand* the shrewd man of material self-interest wins the day and indicates the end of the old dispensation. Within the context of the action it is significant that Cuchulain does not set upon Conchubar in revenge for the part he has played. In his helpless rage he strikes out at life itself, the sea, decapitating the waves, on each of which we are told he sees Conchubar's crown. Having fallen away from the heroic ideal, it is inevitable that experience defeats Cuchulain. In the end he is mastered by the waves but not before that wild assertive gesture has re-established his original heroic stature and confirmed him as a classically tragic figure.

The two scenes which make up the main plot of the play do not exist alone however, and whatever meaning they express is echoed and reinforced by a parallel and representative sequence of action involving a blind man and fool. Like the Elizabethan subplot, such secondary but related material juxtaposes different layers of meaning and encourages the audience to perceive for themselves the different relationships which are brought into being by the multiplicity of characters and actions. The blind man is Conchubar's antiself, both as a vulgar or peasant figure and the negative aspect of the high king's assertion of logic and mean self-interest. Conchubar is blind to the consequences of his actions. In the same way the fool is an exact counterpart to Cuchulain, an anti-heroic figure whose spontaneity and intuition is wholly removed from the practical control of experience. The reliance of the blind man and fool on one another's capacities is emphasised in the play while that between Conchubar and Cuchulain is merely implied, yet the parallelism between the two plots is exact. Conchubar forces his will on Cuchulain and uses him to protect the state while Cuchulain loses his only son because of it. The 'blind' man commands the 'fool' and uses him to protect the state while Cuchulain loses his only son because of it. The real blind man commands the fool and uses him to steal food, but eats up the roasted chicken himself, leaving the fool with nothing for his pains. Lest the point be missed the first woman states that life drifts between a blind man and a fool just before the second entrance of those characters, and so emphasises the wider symbolism of the action as well. The negative qualities of the heroic archetypes are also contrasted with their counterparts by involving the blind man and fool in action which is essentially comic and inconsequential, compared with the high seriousness and importance of actions in the heroic world. The disinterested heroism of Cuchulain and its tragic consequences gain in force by comparison with the ignoble and comic. The inclusion of a contrasting relationship between venal and heroic characters certainly emphasises the dialectical nature of the theme, but it is also useful in establishing dramatic tension. At the beginning of the play the blind man reveals the challenger's identity to both the fool and audience, establishing the central conflict of the action as a dramatic irony. At the end he also reveals the truth to Cuchulain and within this frame the action takes place on several levels simultaneously. It is not just a question of the difference between the character's view of the action and that of the audience, but also of the comparison and contrast between the actual anti-heroic world and the heroic ideal. The consequence of the fall from heroic tradition is demonstrated in the world of the blind man and fool which frames the main action and mediates between it and the world of the audience. The effectiveness of the dramatic device is obvious and the same framing technique is used again in the later dance plays to great advantage, but instead of a parallel plot and secondary characters, a chorus is generally substituted.

On Baile's Strand also makes use of a chorus, but its only function is to intensify the oath which marks the turning point of the main action. Instead of blind man and fool intervening at that point, a chorus of three women sing in low voices, but according to Yeats's instructions, their words should be little more than a murmur under the speeches of the men which continue throughout. The words of the song constitute a traditional rite of exorcism, ensuring that the oath will be adhered to by cancelling out any possibility of malevolent supernatural influence. The words themselves were not of great importance to Yeats, but the ritual gesture of the women, bearing bowls of fire and casting a magic spell, implies the presence of supernatural forces which are significant in the context of the subsequent action. The assertion that Cuchulain's opposition to Conchubar is the work of witches is made believable by the exorcism of antagonistic spirits and the sacerdotal nature of the chorus establishes a pattern of supernatural images which dominates the second half of the play. The chorus is also used to raise dramatic tension by prophesying Cuchulain's downfall as a vision seen in the ashes of the sacred fire and introducing the related figures of blind man and fool who close the action.

Both the chorus of women and the characters of the antithetical action which frames the plot are given songs which parallel their actions and mark off the major subdivisions of the play. The fool sings twice towards the end of the opening scene and again at the beginning of the last. The first song, 'Witches that steal the milk' (Yeats, 1966, p. 469), stresses the supernatural, while the second celebrates Cuchulain's supreme command of both the natural and supernatural world. The third acknowledges him to have become a withered old block and measures the change against the consistency of the fool's nature. The shortened line-lengths of three accented syllables are made even more lyrical by the use of metrical inversion in the first song and of triple metre in the second, while the more emphatic and solemn movement of the tetrameters employed for the women's incantation also expresses their nature and function.

Fool. Cuchulain has killed kings,
  Kings and sons of kings,
  Dragons out of the water,
  And witches out of the air. (p. 467)

Women. May this fire have driven out
  The Shape-Changers that can put
  Ruin on a great king's house
  Until all be ruinous. (p. 495)

Fool. When you were an acorn on the tree-top,
    Then was I an eagle-cock;
  Now that you are a withered old block,
    Still am I an eagle-cock. (p. 519)

The antithetical themes of the play are also expressed through the contrasts of language used by the two different groups of characters. The blind man and fool invariably speak prose while the heroic figures use verse, except for Cuchulain in the last scene who also speaks in prose. The speeches of the blind man and fool are sharply divided into short phrases and sentences giving them more of the repeating rhythm of verse than is common in random speech, yet there is little attempt to use the inflections or locutions of Gaelic-influenced English. Their speech is almost neutral so far as time and place is concerned, yet remains natural and gay by virtue of its shortened sense-units and freely varied rhythms.

  Blind Man. No hurry, no hurry. I know whose son it is. I
    wouldn't tell anybody, but I will tell you, – a secret is better
    to you than your dinner. You like being told secrets. (p. 469)

The heroic speeches of the protagonists in blank verse are much more formal and weighty, and they too remain free from the conscious Irishness of a peasant dialect.

  Cuchulain. It's time the years put water in my blood
    And drowned the wildness in it, for all's changed,
    But that unchanged, – I'll take what oath you will:
    The moon, the sun, the water, light, or air,
    I do not care how binding. (p. 493)

Cuchulain's speeches in prose at the end of the play have very nearly the same rhythmic qualities as those of the blind man and fool and they serve to indicate his fallen nature as well as to preserve the unity of the scene. The contrasting styles reflect the dialectics of the theme, at the same time the various levels of language are ordered and harmonised into a rhythmic movement or pattern which rises and falls with the action and establishes a corresponding emotional response.

The imagery of the play also functions as a reinforcement of the antithetical characters and levels of action. The chicken over which the blind man and fool contest is paralleled by Aoife's tender young son over whom Conchubar and Cuchulain quarrel. The relationship is emphasised by the repeated images of hawk and hawk feathers which are later contrasted with the roasted chicken and other feathers the fool twines in his hair or Cuchulain uses to clean his sword of his son's blood. Cuchulain announces himself to be the son of the hawk, claiming to be the child of a supernatural father and a human mother. He commends the young man's courage by saying that he has shown the hawk's grey feather. Because of the boy's resemblance to his mother, Cuchulain wishes to protect him and insists that the boy's wild challenge is proof enough of his valour; there is no need to test him further. He offers the boy an arm ring as testimony of his friendship and a magical cloak given him by his supernatural father and by which token Aoife and all her people will know of their friendship. The supernatural element here is again important in that the history of the cloak is tied up with the challenge to battle Cuchulain's father offered him, presumably as a test. The father revealed his identity before they crossed swords, however, and sparing Cuchulain, gave him the cloak woven by the women of the country-under-wave. The offer of ring and cloak is repeated and the parallelism of the two challenges is thus insisted upon. The line of heroic descent is very clear; Cuchulain and the culture he represents is at the point of intersection of the natural and supernatural worlds. His son is born wholly within the framework of the natural world but he is no less heroic than his father. As the natural world moves farther and farther away from the heroic ideal, succumbing more and more to pettiness and self-interest, there comes a point when the pattern is broken. In the case of Cuchulain, his instinctive desire to protect and befriend his son is as much to blame for the break with heroic tradition as Conchubar's wish to tame Cuchulain for the sake of peace in his kingdom and the succession of his children. Cuchulain's association with the chicken feathers of the antiplot is no more coincidental than his use of prose in the same scene. Because of his own actions, he and the world he represents have fallen from the heroic ideal and continue on their inevitable course between opposite conditions of absolute being.

The chicken feathers, arm ring, and cloak are all physically present on the stage, but none of them is central enough to attract sufficient attention to itself during performance. The cloak, for example, would have to resemble the wings of a hawk in order that the point be made conclusively, and it would also have to be worn by Cuchulain in the last scene in order to contrast with the chicken feathers. Even then, a very large number of feathers would be needed to make the gesture conspicuous and further emphasis might be gained by allowing the cloak to slip to the floor from Cuchulain's shoulders as he wipes the sword and goes to the door to throw the feathers away. Actually, there is not much reliance on extraliterary devices of stage production and the drama is primarily literary as in the Elizabethan theatre where language appeals directly to the imagination of the audience. Yeats certainly conceived of the actions in terms of the Elizabethan theatre conditions which William Poel was doing so much to revive at that time.

'On Baile's Strand', though produced for the first time at the opening of the Abbey Theatre in December 1904, was planned when I had no hope of that, or any, theatre, and the characters walk on to an empty stage at the beginning and leave that stage empty at the end, because I thought of its performance upon a large platform with a door at the back and an exit through the audience at the side, and no proscenium, or curtain; and being intended for a platform and a popular audience. (p. 1306)

The realistic presentation of a closely structured sequence of action certainly helps to make *On Baile's Strand* a popular play. Its tragicomic qualities offer another reason for its popularity as well as the universal appeal of conflicts between father and son, individual freedom and social conformity. On the other hand, the piece could easily be transformed into a dance play, climaxed by Cuchulain fighting the waves, a dance that was later used to introduce a revised version of *The Only Jealousy of Emer*. The one anti-illusionistic element in the play as we know it is the use of masks for the blind man and fool. The effect is to depersonalise the characters and render them more obviously representative, to place more emphasis on their symbolic nature as both counterparts to Conchubar and Cuchulain and paradigms of universal processes. The ritual fire carried by the chorus of women is also a striking theatrical effect but the symbolism is natural and immediately understood; that of the blind man and fool requires definition by association and stylisation before it can be accepted.

THE ONLY JEALOUSY OF EMER (1919)

Original Publication: Chicago, Dundrum, and London, 1919
First Performance: Amsterdam, 1922

Although the situations and actions of the play are quite clear, their motivation and meaning is not always easy to explain. As is the case with many of the poems written at about the same time, *The Only Jealousy of Emer* is based upon a number of Yeats's convictions about history, human personality, and the supernatural world which he was then arranging into a philosophical system. Esoteric lore, however, ought not to dominate our understanding of the play, but rather the actions and character relationships themselves should suggest an interpretation. The play is primarily about the ambiguity of love, of individual incompleteness and the need for fulfilment by uniting with a complementary being outside oneself. The central situation presents Cuchulain as a pawn rather than an active hero who is no longer in control of his fate. He is unconscious, dead to the temporal world, while his spirit is being seduced into an eternal embrace, a mystical union, with an archetypal female figure or moon goddess. Rather than affirming or celebrating such a union as in *The Shadowy Waters*, *The Only Jealousy of Emer* demonstrates the inevitability and rightness of Cuchulain's rescue from the world of pure spirit. Unlike Mary Bruin in *The Land of Heart's Desire* or Michael Gillane in *Cathleen ni Houlihan*, Cuchulain is prevented from union with the supernatural and returned to a temporal world where he is reunited with Eithne

Inguba. In both cases he is lost to Emer, his once-beloved mate who is forced to renounce his love in order to return him to temporal existence. The terrible irony of her predicament is perhaps the most striking aspect of the play. Theoretically, her choice is of no great matter since Cuchulain will be in someone else's arms no matter what she does. It may be that as the object of her love, she would rather have him alive and close by, even if with another woman, than dead and wholly removed to the perfection of a supernatural existence. But it is also true that both she and the figure of Cuchulain (Bricriu) act on the unspoken assumption that the temporal world, for all its tribulations, is the more attractive and fulfilling of the two. Even Cuchulain resists Fand's blandishments with a very real nostalgia for the intricacies of human remorse. In many ways *The Only Jealousy of Emer* is an affirmation of joy and necessity in human existence while it also recognises the tribulations and declining strength of the individual who is passing from the moment of his greatness to his inevitable end.

Emer's choice and its significance for Cuchulain is fairly easily perceived but her relationship to Eithne Inguba and Fand, the objects of Cuchulain's desire, is another matter. Their main characteristic is perfection of physical beauty, a tender girl and a statuesque goddess, who are manifestations of the same ideal, one in the temporal and the other in the supernatural world. Emer is their opposite, a passionate heroine and woman of action, the incarnation of a sun goddess and rightful mate to the youthful Cuchulain. There is certainly ample evidence in the text that Eithne Inguba is frail and timid, she must be forced into action by the more robust and decisive Emer while the woman of the sidhe is fragile and exquisite, a figure on the very brink of spiritual fulfilment which will annihilate forever the self-consciousness of thought and memory. Emer, on the other hand, enters into a struggle with the circumstances of her life and so maintains the heroic ideal. It is right and natural for her to rescue Cuchulain who has been overcome by life. The magic sleep in which we find him is linked directly to his heroic fight with the sea in *On Baile's Strand* and the scene is laid in a fisherman's house nearby. Cuchulain's body has only recently been rescued from the sea which had overcome him. The Cuchulain of *The Green Helmet* who establishes his right to the champion's crown by defying death for the sake of honour has been overcome as a result of his lapse from the heroic ideal. The present stage or turning point in his life's cycle is the second confrontation with the supernatural but now it is he who is pursued rather than pursuing. The young man who set out to hood the hawk woman of the air in *At the Hawk's Well* is now middle-aged and helpless before the moon goddess.

The three manifestations of Cuchulain are also related to one another in very nearly the same way, and so form a pattern which closely corresponds to that of the three women. The real Cuchulain who is the coveted object of the conflict falls into Eithne Inguba's arms on being restored to life, seeking reassurance and human comfort. The ghost of Cuchulain is an almost passive figure who exists only in the supernatural world but ultimately rejects Fand's insistent seduction. The figure of Cuchulain is their opposite or antiself but in a double sense, not merely the counterpart in an antithetical sphere or quality of existence, supernatural rather than temporal, but also an inversion of the primary qualities that Cuchulain represents. Bricriu's antagonism is a negation of Cuchulain's magnanimity; his nature is a distortion of the ideal and this is reflected in the physical characteristics which distinguish him from Cuchulain. Like Fand who exists only in the supernatural world and manifests herself in *At the Hawk's Well* by possessing the guardian, he possesses Cuchulain's body but his face is grotesque and his arm withered. Bricriu of the sidhe in this play is obviously related to Cuchulain's earlier antagonist, the red man of *The Green Helmet* and Conchubar (the blind man) of *On Baile's Strand*. He represents a personality type, the hunchback, which Yeats placed towards the last of the phases of the moon on the great wheel, just before the return to complete objectivity. The figure of Cuchulain (Bricriu) is very nearly opposite in nature to Fand, Eithne Inguba, and even Cuchulain, who is now in the most completely subjective phase of his progress through life. The figure of Cuchulain is physically distorted and ugly, for example, as opposed to the perfect beauty of the two subjective manifestations, and Bricriu's actions are motivated by a desire to thwart Fand's end and prevent Cuchulain from escaping the cycle of generation. His unexplained quarrel with the woman of the sidhe is understandable when seen in this light as is the motivation for his relationship with Emer.

A question remains; why should Emer be required to renounce Cuchulain's love in order to save him from Fand's embrace? The text offers us no explicit help, any more than it explains why Bricriu is Fand's enemy, and we can only surmise that motivation as such is unimportant or that it is implicit in the action. The supernatural must seek to complete itself by union with the natural world and man must strive to reunite himself with the supernatural. Individuals progress through cycles of development which are determined by opposite states of being, over and over again, until they have so perfected their natures as to warrant an escape into non-being. The force and thrust of objective or primary states of being are inimical to the tendency towards subjectivity and tend to prevent the exit of individuals from the cycle. Emer's renunciation is as much a ritual acknowledgement that Cuchulain's progress through the cycle has brought about a permanent estrangement between them as it is an act of heroic self-sacrifice and magnanimity which brings about his resurrection from the dead. Emer is jealous. She does suffer and yet she meets her own fate in the full knowledge and acceptance of its necessity. The key to the situation is Cuchulain's hesitation in uniting with the woman of the sidhe. He has not achieved the needed passionlessness to merge with the timeless; he is tainted by memory and remorse which cause him to call out to Emer just as he is about to embrace Fand. Both on the human level and the symbolic, Emer's renunciation is justified, even knowing as she does, that when he wakes, he will never return to her arms.

The myth which served as Yeats's source, 'The Sickbed of Cuchulain', the last part of which is also known as 'The Only Jealousy of Emer', offers an effective measure of the originality in his play of the same name. According to Lady Gregory's version, Cuchulain's magic sleep is an enchantment put upon him by Fand who has been abandoned by Manannon, her husband, and wishes to take Cuchulain as her lover. He goes to her quite readily and when Emer learns of their trysting place, she sets out with her handmaidens to kill Fand. Cuchulain's loyalties are put to the test and at one point he tells Emer that she will always find favour in his eyes. Fand defers to Emer in order to save face and the situation is rescued by the appearance of Manannon to whom Fand reluctantly returns. The very physical Cuchulain of the legend, whom even a goddess desires, is transformed by Yeats into a metaphysical archetype while a scheme of complex relationships and dynamic conflict is created as a paradigm of the universal forces which determine both human personality and history. The warrior hero of the *Táin Bó Cúalnge* has become the acknowledged representative of a mystical-occult system. Yeats's romantic belief in the corporeal reality of imagination, dream, or image and in the dreaming back of the dead through their life-time experience in expiation of their passions, is a basic assumption of the play. The imagery and character oppositions are taken from the great wheel of lunar phases which reached its most complete expression in *A Vision* (1937). It has often been suggested that the action of *The Only Jealousy of Emer* is also autobiographical and that is very generally true of all Yeats's work, but an identification of the individual roles with the various women in Yeats's life isn't going to help very much towards an understanding of the wider implications and symbolism of the play. Even if the characters and actions are closely related to the author's life, real or imagined, it is also true that all human existence follows the dialectical pattern outlined in the play. That larger pattern is undoubtedly the one which Yeats is at pains to present, especially in the plays comprising the cycle of Cuchulain's life. *The Only Jealousy of Emer* is not only related directly to the action of *On Baile's Strand* through the explicit linking of Cuchulain's unconsciousness or death to his fight with the sea, but also to *The Green Helmet* in its insistence on Emer as a complementary solar figure. It is also connected to *At the Hawk's Well* in the explicit identification of Fand as the hawk-woman of the air who had eluded Cuchulain in his aggressive youth. Now that the hero has reached the point in his development which is characterised by the greatest subjectivity, the woman of the sidhe desires him for her own spiritual fulfilment. In Cuchulain's case the gesture is premature. He is not ready for ultimate union with the supernatural and he is called back to life in order to complete the natural cycle of being, to assimilate fully the mask of his earlier self.

The scene between the ghost of Cuchulain and the woman of the sidhe is the very heart of the play. It is antithetical to the scene between Emer and the figure of Cuchulain (Bricriu), and provides a gloss on that earlier scene. Whereas the possession of the body of Cuchulain by Bricriu of the sidhe introduces a supernatural element and raises the level of dramatic tension, the appearance of a goddess whose costume suggests a piece of metal sculpture dancing seductively before a phantom is calculated to magnify the effect still farther. The transition from the very down-to-earth dialogue between Eithne Inguba and Emer to a direct representation of supernatural experience is smoothly accomplished and the climactic nature of the scene within a scene is confirmed by the startling shift of verse form. From the very beginning of his career as a dramatist, Yeats had alternated heroic blank verse with lesser elevated registers or styles and punctuated or framed the action with more intensely lyrical songs. In this play he needed language which would cut above heroic speech and indicate action on a purely spiritual plane. The solution was to shorten the line length slightly, enforce a less freely varied metrical regularity and add approximate rhyme in successive couplets rather than alternate lines. The contrast of elements produces very subtle effects. For example, the formal regularity of the tetrameters is balanced by the rapidity of return and musicality of the shorter line while the couplet rhymes hint at a superhuman stylisation which is softened by their partial nature and the fact that the sense units and sentences run on from line to line without relation to the rhyme.

> *Woman of the Sidhe.* Could you that have loved many a woman
>   That did not reach beyond the human,
>   Lacking a day to be complete,
>   Love one that, though her heart can beat,
>   Lacks it but by an hour or so? (Yeats, 1966, p. 553)

On the other hand the heroic blank verse of the other characters is rather unremarkable and not very different from the style which Yeats had been using for some years. At one and the same time they are elevated in rhythm and diction without losing flexibility and naturalness.

> *Emer.*   And so that woman
>   Has hid herself in this disguise and made
>   Herself into a lie.

> *Figure of Cuchulain.*   A dream is body;
>   The dead move ever towards a dreamless youth
>   And when they dream no more return no more;
>   And those more holy shades that never lived
>   But visit you in dreams. (p. 549)

The lyrics sung and spoken by the chorus are another matter entirely. The first is written for a single voice and is based on a tetrameter line. It includes the occasional pentameter for contrast, however, and intensifies to trimeters in order to suggest climax. The final song is given by a chorus of three voices and further heightens the emotional tension. In keeping with the general acceleration and compounding of effects throughout the play, the basic verse form is trimeter which gives way to dimeters and occasional tetrameters. The rhythmic pattern or movement thus created opens with lines of four stresses in which both imagery and a context of action is established. The verse form then changes to lines of five stresses in the scenes between Eithne Inguba and Emer as well as in the dialogue that follows between Emer and Bricriu. The rhythm then mounts in tension to the lines of four stresses in the scene between Cuchulain's ghost and Fand, returning to five for the resolution of the action and ends with the extremely flexible and lyrical lines of three stresses in which the significant imagery of the play and its major theme is re-emphasised. The songs for the folding and unfolding of the cloth which replace the conventional curtain of a proscenium stage have caused a good deal of controversy as to their interpretation, but the references they contain bear a reasonably straightforward relationship to the main action.

In the opening song, 'A woman's beauty is like a white/ Frail bird' (p. 529), a sea bird has been struck down from the air to the dark soil of the regenerating earth and an exquisite shell has been cast up by the troubled sea onto the loud sand. Both are said to be images of loveliness which have come into being through processes of toil and suffering over long periods of time. In the play there are two figures of exquisite beauty; Eithne Inguba, Cuchulain's concubine who is warmly physical and human, and the woman of the sidhe, Cuchulain's desire, who is the perfect form of a labyrinthine ideal. After the speech in which the setting is described, the first musician sings the words that the bitter sea cries out to the bird and shell, telling them that it would not take as friend so weak and unserviceable a thing as man. Cuchulain is, of course, the man who drifts and dreams while Eithne Inguba and Fand represent slightly differentiated aspects of a single stage in human development. Eithne Inguba is the mortal manifestation closest to incarnation at phase fifteen, which is that of immortal beauty at the point of perfect subjectivity and is represented in the play by Fand. According to the imagery of *A Vision*, the sea bird is associated with the full moon while the hawk is associated with phase one, the dark of the moon or the supernatural incarnation of perfect objectivity. The woman of the sidhe in *At the Hawk's Well* is also Fand, but in an opposite manifestation, and her human counterpart at that point on the great wheel is the warrior, Aoife. Just as Cuchulain pursues and overcomes Aoife at the end of the earlier play, he finds himself in Eithne Inguba's arms at the end of *The Only Jealousy of Emer*. As he progresses through the destined cycle, always seeking other loves (masks) in order to complete himself, Emer, his natural mate, always finds favour in his eyes.

The first stanza of the final chorus, 'Why does your heart beat thus,' (p. 563) appears to be addressed to the audience by the musicians who face them and sympathise with the natural reaction of fear induced by an unexpected encounter with the supernatural. The stanza ends with a compassionate plea for the release of such a spirit into nonexistence. It is more probable, however, that the rhetorical question is asked of Fand, for it is she who is the phantom with a beating heart on the threshold of an ultimate exit from existence. That interpretation is indeed confirmed in stanza three where the inevitability of her success is questioned. Even though she has escaped mortal existence and is now incarnated as pure spirit, even though no man can withhold his desire for her, the final step into eternity is not a foregone conclusion. The man himself may not be ready and so turn from the supernatural image she has become to a more human breast. This is, of course, exactly what happens in the play. The fifth stanza implies that since the subjective ideal has not been fulfilled, the image passes through the rest of the cycles where there is further danger of choosing a complementary mask badly and so falling further away from perfect unity of being. When the moon is in its final stages, that is from phase twenty-two to twenty-eight, the stars are dimmed and out of sight and the subjective ideal is then wholly guided by her mate (mask). The final chorus tells us as much about Yeats's system as it does about the play, and together with the opening lyrics focuses our attention on the centrality of Eithne Inguba and Fand and away from any psychological and human interest we may have in Emer or her plight.

Another image pattern or motif which tends to confirm the idea that Emer is one of several agents in the symbolic scheme of the play is the kiss with which Eithne Inguba summons the shape-changing Bricriu, the unconsummated kiss between Fand and the ghost of Cuchulain, and the final embrace between Eithne Inguba and the restored Cuchulain. Emer's renunciation merely substitutes Eithne Inguba's kiss for Fand's. It does not alter the object of Cuchulain's desire, but rather the level or plane of his fulfilment. Emer is the instrument for restoring Cuchulain to temporal existence with all its joys and sorrows and she is a necessary symbolic figure in the dramatic scheme of universal forces. Her heroic sacrifice is certainly emphasised by the final irony of Eithne Inguba's claim that she alone has rescued Cuchulain from the sea. In terms of the play's imagery Emer (sun or objectivity) is associated with the hearth fire which is antithetical to all sea imagery (moon or subjectivity), including both bird and shell. Emer tends the flame at the beginning of the play because the enchantments of the sea are exorcised by fire and at the same time draws the bed curtains to shield Cuchulain's face from the image (the sea) which has brought him to his present crisis. During the attempts of Eithne Inguba to recall him to life, Emer stands at the imaginary fire, warming herself, and her actions are even further accented by musical accompaniment. Imagery and production method can hardly be distinguished from one another at this point but the effect and its significance is fairly clear.

As in the case of *At the Hawk's Well*, Yeats conceived the play for performance in a private house or public room and not for a conventional stage. In both the manner of presentation and plot construction he had the Japanese nōh in mind and wished for a private and intellectually committed audience. Extra-literary features such as masks, musical accompaniment, and dancing were introduced to add further dimensions of meaning and to establish a new relationship between the audience and the dramatic action. The symbolic situations of the play are brought into the real world of the audience, not distanced from it by stage illusionism and a darkened auditorium. Costumes, properties, and chorus also help to emphasise the archetypal nature of actions which are obviously those of dream or imagination, but have been rendered physical or real by being acted out. The play, as we have it, is not very closely related to the Japanese nōh, even though there is some evidence that its structure was influenced by the text of *Aoi no Ue* which Yeats knew from the Ezra Pound – Ernest Fenollosa translation. In that play Prince Genji's wife lies unconscious upon her sick-bed and suffers the vicious attacks of Lady Rokujo's incarnated jealousy. Aoi no Ue's rival is her husband's lover. The dynamics of dialectical themes and presentation are common to both plays, but instead of imitating the nōh, Yeats created a new dramatic form, a lyrical theatre or drama of ideas and intense emotions whose ordering principle is a patterning of images and rhythms rather than a logical and realistic plot.

THE HOUR-GLASS (1914)

Original Publication: Boston and London, 1903
First Performance: Dublin, 1903

In terms of its original conception and first publication, *The Hour-Glass* belongs to the period of *The King's Threshold*, but Yeats revised it substantially some ten years later, recasting the dialogue in verse and introducing experimental features of stage production. The play is little more than a simple moral fable and the action is not very different from that of a medieval morality play. *Everyman* had been very successfully revised by the Elizabethan Stage Society only a few years before and its combination of allegorical representation and doctrinal advocacy would naturally appeal to Yeats who founded his own plot on a tale from Lady Wilde's *Ancient Legends, Mystic Charms and Superstitions of Ireland* (1887). *The Hour-Glass* follows its source fairly closely even to the final image of the butterfly, but he introduces the figure of the fool as dramatic counterpart to the wise man as well as elements of his own philosophic world-view.

Yeats's fool is a figure out of folklore, a holy fool, rather than Shakespeare's sophisticated foil. He is a natural force and an expression of imagination, joy, and spontaneity who is readily associated with the supernatural world and who functions through subjective insight or intuition rather than through objective reasoning or logic. The fool of *The Hour-Glass* lives on the frontier between the temporal and supernatural world. He experiences modes of existence which reason and empirical judgement deny. The almost allegorical nature of his character is obvious as is that of the wise man, and the natural opposition which exists between them constitutes the dramatic conflict of the play. By logical argument and reason the wise man has convinced everyone with whom he has come into contact that nothing exists which cannot be seen or touched. He is, however, confronted by the supernatural world which he has so long denied and his salvation depends on finding one person who still believes in the supernatural despite his own teaching. The fool is that man, he is necessary to the wise man's salvation and the play seems to be saying that the wise man must grow to resemble the fool in order to perfect his own character and enter into the kingdom of pure spirit.

There is no doubt as to the wise man's conversion to belief in the supernatural. The apparition of the angel is quite enough to convince him on the instant. His one thought is to find the believer who will save him from eternal torment. Throughout the second half of the play he tries vainly to wring a confession of belief from his pupils, his wife, his children, and Teigue, the fool, in order to avoid his doom. Had any one of them been able to save him from the torments of hell, however, the real point of the play as we now have it, would be lost. When Teigue goes out without having saved him, the wise man is shocked into a right understanding of universal order.

> We perish into God and sink away
> Into reality – the rest's a dream.
>
> (Yeats, 1966, p. 635)

The only reality is in putting aside selfhood and the temporal manifestations of existence, which is seen as a merging with god and therefore entering into non-existence. Life and even the torments of damnation are only a dream. When the fool returns, ready to answer the wise man's questions and save him from hell, the wise man stops him, knowing that there is no significant difference between existence in the body and that in hell. The wise man has made an intellectual leap forward through a crisis of the spirit and become as the fool, perceiving and accepting the dialectical forces of universal order and entrusting himself confidently to the providence and justice of that order. Like so many of Yeats's heroes and heroines, the wise man perfects his own character through his self-conscious sacrifice. He achieves beatitude by denying selfhood and merging with an antithetical principle. In the same way the character relationships are very similar to others found in Yeats's plays. The fool is closely related to Seanchan, for example, and certainly to Cuchulain, while the wise man, as a principle of the mind, can be associated with King Guaire, the red man, Conchubar, or Bricriu of the sidhe. The great strength of *The Hour-Glass* is the directness and lucidity of the symbolism and also the clear exposition and acceptability of its more esoteric philosophy.

The Christian element in the play is carefully balanced by the wider context of folk belief, vision and superstition. The text chosen by the pupils is one which the wise man has twice encountered in recent dreams and he is unnerved by the coincidence. Dramatic expectation is thus raised and also confirmed by the fool's personal experience of a circumambient supernatural world which is more Celtic and intimate in its manifestations than Roman Catholic and formal. The dialogue which follows establishes a conflict or oppositions of interests, and the entrance of the angel again raises the level of action and excitement to a new pitch which reaches a climax at its exit. Supernatural manifestations are real, whether the bleating of fairy lambs in November or the visitations of angels. In one of its last speeches the angel answers the wise man's rationalisations as to the naturalness of human doubt which is based on empirical evidence such as sickness and death, physical corruption or floods and droughts. The doctrinal point is as valid for Christianity as it is for mystical-occult systems: the soul is meant to rise above the limitations of physical existence. Deprivation, pain, and death are nothing to the immortal soul which joyfully proclaims its own virtues. The action of the second half of the play fills in the gap between this speech and the wise man's independent realisation of its validity with actions which both entertain and reinforce our understanding of the seriousness and effects of the wise man's folly. The pupils romp about and laugh at the wise man's passionate protestations, Brigit is a suitably naive foil, and the children are of no use at all. Teigue is the only serious hope, and yet when the wise man attempts to pray and discovers that he has forgotten his Latin, he laments that he will have to pray in the common tongue like a clown begging in public or Teigue the fool. Through Teigue's example, however, the wise man comes to discover humility and wins salvation by submitting himself wholly to god's will. His death is a perfect example of tragic joy, a happy and purposeful melting together of opposites.

The language of the play is as straightforward and uncomplicated as its characters and plot. A very neutral and natural blank verse alternates with rhythmic prose throughout, establishing both elevated and contrasting tones. The diction as well as the syntax of the lines varies little between the wise man and pupils when they are being serious, while Brigit and the fool are given a more colloquial turn of phrase derived from peasant dialect, as are the pupils when they are playing about. Neither Brigit, the children, nor yet the fool speak in verse, while the angel speaks consistently in a very regular and formal verse form.

> *Angel.* Only when all the world has testified,
> May soul confound it, crying out in joy,
> And laughing on its lonely precipice.
> What's dearth and death and sickness to the soul
> That knows no virtue but itself? Nor could it,
> So trembling with delight and mother-naked,
> Live unabashed if the arguing world stood by. (p. 603)

The wise man and pupils alternate between prose and verse, yet the prose is not always so easily distinguishable from verse because the natural rhythms of the sense units approximate blank verse.

> *Wise Man.* The beggar who wrote that on Babylon wall meant that there is a spiritual kingdom that cannot be seen or known till the faculties, whereby we master the kingdom of this world, wither away like green things in winter. A monkish thought, the most mischievous thought that ever passed out of a man's mouth. (p. 585)

The play begins in prose, shifting into verse at the passionate moment when the wise man becomes aware of the implications of the text the pupils have chosen. The first speech is a very marked contrast to the prose because of its shorter line lengths tetrameters accented with trimeters. The second speech moves back towards normal pentameters, even though it too is accented by brief and intense tetrameters. Verse is not used again until the wise man's climactic speech to the fool which also introduces the angel. Here too, emphasis is gained by contrasting colloquial pentameters with passionate trimeters. The dialogue between the wise man and angel is more elevated and formal as befits the gravity of their discourse, and the dramatic tension is broken abruptly by the pupils who enter singing and dancing about the fool. The jolly song, 'Who stole your wits away' (pp. 605 and 607), is played off against the argumentation in Latin between the wise man and pupils which shows that, in a sense, he has stolen their mother-wit away. Blank verse is the predominant form of the speeches. Brigit's entrance in an apron and with her bare arms covered in flour, reintroduces prose while her husband continues in verse and the contrast of forms is carried through the dialogue between wise man and fool to the very end of the play. The wise man's final speech is a very subtle realisation of effects, combining the varied line lengths used throughout with sound echoes and occasional rhyme words.

> *Wise Man.* Be silent. May God's will prevail on the instant,
> Although His will be my eternal pain,
> I have no question:
> It is enough, I know what fixed the station
> Of star and cloud.
> And knowing all, I cry
> That whatso God has willed
> On the instant be fulfilled,
> Though that be my damnation. (p. 637)

Even the fool's last speech includes the contrastive touch of the three-line lyric in trimeters, 'I hear the wind a-blow' (p. 639), which underlines once again the importance of intuitive understanding. The variations in language and verse form which give the action an expressive rhythmic structure is given further stress as it rises to its first musical climax in the speeches of the angel. Yeats wanted the angel to speak on pure musical notes set down beforehand and rehearsed so that the quality of a plain-song (Gregorian) chant might contrast with the more random and passionate speeches of the wise man. *The Hour-Glass* is certainly one of Yeats's more interesting experiments in the integration of lyrical and dramatic effects.

Images also play a large part in the patterning of the

composition outside the obvious instance of the characters themselves as allegorical figures or archetypes. The hourglass, however, is the only one which really has a physical reality of its own. It is visible on stage throughout and reminds the audience of the temporal nature of the action. The image becomes of major importance when the angel turns it over and announces the imminence of the wise man's death. Practically all the other images are verbal and are associated with either the objective rationality of the wise man or the subjective intuition of the fool. For example, the references to Babylon carry with them the connotations of scientific rationalism being engulfed by mysterious and unxplainable forces of the supernatural world. The occult text chosen by the pupils for discussion was written upon the walls of Babylon and the wise man argues that the Babylonian moon would blot everything out should the supernatural messengers standing in the fiery cloud be questioned. In the next breath he claims that when cold intellect is fired, melts and fumes, it manifests itself as the figure of god in the Babylonian furnace with Shadrak, Meshak and Abednego. A related image is that of a personified frenzy who beats his drum as reason grows dim and impels even the wise man to dance to his tune. The idea of a spiritual crisis and direct revelation is taken up again at the entrance of the angel and repeated at Brigit's exit when the wise man asserts that the soul may find truth in a flash on the battlefield or amid overwhelming waves. The repetition of images prepares the audience for his own crisis at the end of the play and the spiritual truth he perceives.

The images most closely associated with the fool and the supernatural irrationality he represents are those of the eagle and hawk. The very first scene has Teigue spread-eagled, holding the huge book on his back like a brass lectern in a Christian church. The angel, his spiritual counterpart, is associated with frenzy which has swooped down like a hawk and is later said to have appeared suddenly like a hawk out of the air. Other ideas of the subjective and supernatural intervention which is the point of the play are represented by the meaninglessness of a jester's rattle, dried peas in a bladder or pod, and yet again, with the naturalness and omnipresence of grass. Perhaps the most striking image is that of the net which Teigue claims men use to catch angels and that which god loves to fill with the souls of men. Both are related to the very real nets on which the fishermen allow Teigue to sleep because he brings them luck. And the pennies which Teigue begs throughout the play are also closely connected with that luck. The holy fool is a mediator of sorts, offering the assistance of supernatural forces in exchange for the currency of the temporal world, pennies with which to buy food and drink. Teigue's physical needs are the exact counterpart of god's spiritual ones, heaven is empty and those who keep watch there are lonely. The great Fisher's net longs to be filled and because of this, the wise man who has caused an imbalance in the counterpoised forces of the universe must die. Instead of damnation, however, he perceives the truth in the frenzied moment of his struggle for life. His soul's salvation is imaged as a white butterfly being carried away by the angel in a golden casket. What is extraordinary about the images which stress the symbolic scheme of the play is that almost all of them are commonplace and unexceptionable, even to an audience which does not share Yeats's mystical-occult world-view. Whether taken from Christian iconography or folklore, they are quickly established as meaningful within the context of the action. This wider accessibility helps to account for the play's popularity at the Abbey Theatre.

In terms of its production method, on the other hand, *The Hour-Glass* is far from conventional and incorporates some of Yeats's most characteristic theatrical devices. In the stage version of 1912, for example, the framing of the action by the pupils introducing the play from a deep forestage and the fool, also outside the curtain, closing it, suggests that the main action is a play within a play, not an illusion of reality but a stylised presentation whose significance is in some other way analogous to the experience of the audience. The use of a mask for the fool and angel also insists on the characters as principles of the mind rather than real people, while the midpoint of the action is accented by melodic chanting as well as boisterous singing and dancing. The earlier harmonies and associations of the colour scheme were replaced by subtle changes of tone or atmosphere through the interplay of coloured lights on the ivory screens before which the action takes place. Originally, the wise man and pupils were dressed in various shades of purple with tinges of green here and there, the fool and wife in red-brown while the background was an olive-green curtain. The screens designed by Edward Gordon Craig shifted the primary visual effect from colour relationships in which the characters harmonised with their background to one in which the characters were emphasised against a more neutral background by being enveloped in an expressive atmosphere of coloured light. In both cases, however, the settings were meant to project the generalised timelessness characteristic of the original conception. Even in so early and simple a play, Yeats's concern with experimentation and the recreation of action in terms of both theatrical and lyrical composition is readily apparent.

THE UNICORN FROM THE STARS (1908)

Original Publication: New York, 1908
    as WHERE THERE IS NOTHING: Dublin and New York, 1902
First Performance: Dublin, 1907
    as WHERE THERE IS NOTHING: London, 1904

Although certainly not one of Yeats's most characteristic plays, *The Unicorn from the Stars* is a very interesting experiment in its attempt to express a metaphysical idea or scheme through a rather conventional and comic plot. Yeats freely acknowledged Lady Gregory's help in writing a play for which she created characters and dialogue while retaining his original scheme and ideas. The structure of the play is very different from his other work of the same period. Instead of condensation and intensity we have a long and loosely constructed plot which admits of episodes and scenes whose primary concerns are exposition, character development, and atmospheric or comic effect. Rather than the experimental one-act form, which includes only the essential action of a passionate situation, a conventional three-act structure is used as well as the organising principles of classical comedy: exposition, inversion or inflation, catastrophe, recognition or deflation, and resolution. Put very simply, the hero has a vision which calls him away from material pursuits; he misinterprets its meaning and application, introduces anarchy and chaos into a settled society, and then recognises the mistake, but the forces he has unleashed overwhelm him in the end. The scheme is rather unpromising, but the visual and realistic interpolations by Lady

Gregory help a good deal to offset the effect of an almost inhuman central character who is either wrapt in visions of another world or sets about mindlessly overturning this one.

Basically the play is a celebration of the spiritual life and a negation or denial of temporal existence. The idea that the action sets out to exemplify comes from early prose works such as 'Where There is Nothing, There is God' published in *The Secret Rose* (1897) and reprinted in *Mythologies* (1959), or a superseded play entitled *Where There is Nothing* (1902), which is included in *Variorum Plays* (1966), but the scheme of characters and actions is original. Martin Hearne is the subjective hero of the piece who is reaching out towards an objective mask or antiself. He is an artificer or craftsman and a visionary whose very name associates him with water and wading birds. His uncle, Thomas, on the contrary, is a man of practical affairs and pragmatic views, while Andrew is a combination of the two, a reformed or domesticated visionary who still plays the flute and escapes into reverie or vision when he can. Andrew, however, is not a perfected subjective type who, like Martin, might experience a vision of white unicorns. He is sensual and self-indulgent. His weakness is drink and rather than striving after spiritual ecstasy, he is content with physical exhilaration. Each of the three have objective or active counterparts, whose names also serve to associate them together as a group; Father John, Johnny Bocach, and Johnny Gibbons. Father John, like Andrew Hearne, is a lapsed visionary who allowed himself through timidity to be bound to time and traditional religion. He dared not pursue his visions to their logical end, because he lacked Martin's strength and abandon. In him the balance between subjectivity and objectivity had not been struck and Martin lets us know that he perceives the fact when he takes command of the revolt. Johnny Bocach parallels Thomas Hearne as a man of action and worldly concern but with the additional joy and abandon of an objective hero. Led on by Johnny Bocach's mistaken belief that Martin is really Johnny Gibbons, a dashing patriot reported to have returned from exile leading a revolt against British rule in Ireland, Martin misinterprets the vision he only partially remembers and his spiritual quest becomes confused with Johnny Bocach's political goals. As in the other cases, Martin and Johnny Gibbons are exact opposites but through the confusion of their characters and goals, Martin becomes a kind of Johnny Gibbons,

leading an army of inspired thieves and beggars against private
property in an attempt to overthrow law and restore the exaltation
of the heart which had existed in ancient heroic times. Having
thus completed his personality, Martin's death or deliverance
from the human condition is inevitable and provides us with
another example of tragic joy, the merging of opposites into an
ultimate fulfilment.

To a very large extent Martin Hearne is a modern counterpart
or version of Cuchulain and they share several important
features. Martin must be awakened from a state of trance or
vision in which he undergoes a spiritual crisis or moment of
revelation, just as Cuchulain does in *The Only Jealousy of Emer.* The
scheme of character relationships in each play does appear to
parallel the other. By contrast, however, Martin stands out
against the corrupting voice of conventional reason and regains
heroic stature while in *On Baile's Strand* Cuchulain succumbs and
falls away from unity of being. A further echo exists in Johnny
Bocach's lament that some malevolent force or supernatural evil
is striking down the heroes of the Gael and we also recall the
assertion of the kings in *On Baile's Strand* that it was witches who
were causing Cuchulain's strange behaviour. As before, however,
we must look to the reason Yeats offers for the failure of the Gael.
He seems to be suggesting that physical and political destruction
are ineffectual and wrong-headed. Martin, his hero, preaches the
destruction of time and the five senses by which we experience the
created universe. The point of the play is Martin's recognition
that his contribution is revelation, not reformation. Like the wise
man of *The Hour-Glass*, he comes to know that in a fiery moment
of intense passion the mind is free of all thought and experiences a
divine ecstasy. Martin communicates the revelation as he
experiences it and in that fiery moment is shot and killed.
Paudeen's accusation that Biddy misled him with the prophecy
that he was coming to the best day of his life is ambiguous. His
death is the best day of his life. It is its climax and apotheosis.
Only from the point of view of one committed to physical
existence could his death be seen as a loss, and the play itself
directs us to the opposite view.

Unfortunately, Martin's symbolic vision at the end of the play
does not rise above its own rhetoric. There is an inherent
difficulty in expressing its superhuman or spiritual nature
whereas its debased human or temporal image in the earlier

projections of revelry and rapine are more real and moving. The accessibility and effectiveness of the characters, incidents, and language tend to outweigh the more esoteric underpinnings of the play and contribute to its strengths. The use of tramps and thieves as the real inheritors of ancient tradition, heroic ideals, and supernatural lore is immediately acceptable to a popular audience. It is easier to identify and sympathise with familiar low-life characters than with idealised heroic archetypes, and the comic inversions they provide make an even stronger point of contrast with the petty and degraded bourgeoisie Yeats was so fond of satirising. In fact, the tramp has become the archetypal anti-hero of modern European theatre and the representative figure of our time. The development of this very powerful theatrical image can be traced back to Yeats and the work of the early Abbey Theatre.

In the case of *The Unicorn from the Stars* it may be that Lady Gregory is more directly responsible for the creation of the low-life characters. The inclusion of the comic quarrels between Nanny and Biddy Lally, for example, is not typical of Yeats's work, but the realistic ballast this provides is beneficial in the long run. Even the divining scene and Biddy's prophecy is really unnecessary to the action, but again it contributes a needed depth of atmosphere and a supernatural element which lends the action a sense of variety and multiplicity. The outline or shape of the action is also effective, if unremarkable, and the mounting tension arises naturally from the situations themselves. The first act speeds gradually towards the dramatic intervention of Johnny Bocach and the misguided revelation his words bring to Martin. It ends in excitement and expectation which is carried on into the next act where it is further emphasised by the bickering of the old woman, the plan and preparations for war against law and the contrast of Thomas Hearne's outrage. Act two ends in drunken revelry and Martin's commitment to destruction which is realised in setting fire to his own golden coach. The final section begins as an anti-climax on the morning after the sack, with Martin again in trance, but moves rapidly to his inspired vision, beatitude and ultimate death. The symmetry of the construction with first a false and then a valid assertion of meaning and order in the universe, is effective, and especially so with the addition of the enlivening and realistic scenes which intervene. With the exception of incidental music and singing, the plot construction is wholly conventional and the language almost unexceptionally uniform.

The songs are more or less relegated to the middle act and only the ritual prayer in trimeters, 'Rafael keep him Wednesday' (Yeats, 1966, p. 668), appears in act one to accent Johnny Bocach's attempted theft. Johnny sings a melancholy convicts' ballad of three stanzas in act two, 'O come all ye airy bachelors' (p. 679), a kind of dramatic set-piece to introduce variety into the scene and end the bickering of the two old women. Almost immediately after, Paudeen suggests Martin's secret identity through song rather than speech:

> O, Johnny Gibbons, my five hundred healths to you!
> It's long you are away from us over the sea! (p. 680)

and the same device recurs at the beginning of act three as a lament over Martin's seeming death:

> O, Johnny Gibbons, it's you were the prop to us.
> You to have left us, we are foals astray! (p. 694)

At the end of that act as well, another couplet from the song is sung as they carry Martin's body away:

> Our hope and our darling, our heart dies with you:
> You to have failed us, we are foals astray! (p 710)

Two other songs are inserted into the effective unity which has been so carefully created. The first occurs during the climactic scene of rowdy drinking in which a short irregular lyric is boisterously sung while Andrew Hearne adds to the din with his flute: 'O, the lion shall lose his strength.' (p. 690) In its placement and meaning the last example exactly balances the ritual prayer of act one and further emphasises the symmetry of construction. Soon after Nanny croons a macabre rhyme:

> Three that are watching my time to run,
> The worm, the Devil, and my son,
> To see a loop around their neck,
> It's what would make my heart to lep! (p. 696)

Throughout the play the language is very consistent; a

rhythmical prose prevails which ranges through various gradations from the heightened inflections and extravagant metaphors couched in peasant dialect to Martin's more neutral syntax and diction.

> *Martin.* I was mistaken when I set out to destroy Church and Law. The battle we have to fight is fought out in our own mind. There is a fiery moment, perhaps once in a lifetime, and in that moment we see the only thing that matters . . . .
> *Johnny.* The curse of my heart on you! It would be right to send you to your own place on the flagstone of the traitors in Hell. When once I have made an end of you I will be as well satisfied to be going to my death for it as if I was going home! (pp. 704-5)

Passionate intensity of language is achieved by breaking up sentences into shorter and shorter sense units, but also by the repetition of related images.

Gold and silver, sun and moon, day and night are recurring figures but the coach with its golden lion and unicorn is the most important visual image in the play. The coach is the vehicle of life, it is associated here with materialism, commerce, and government. The heraldic lion and unicorn which surmount it are reinterpreted in this play as opposites, an objective and subjective force in conflict. The followers of the unicorn are in strength; the coach is burnt as Thomas Hearne, the honest bourgeois, is seized by them while they sing, 'O, the lion shall loose his strength', before going out to burn and pillage. The painted unicorn on their banner replaces the coach as a central image and both are underscored throughout by continuing references to apocalyptic unicorns which trample and destroy as in the vision of the winepress of the wrath of god from Revelation 14. 20. A related image is the music of clashing swords and of battle which sounds like laughter. The unicorns are more closely related to Yeats's occult studies than to heraldry while the music of joyful laughter and clashing swords first appeared in 'The Death of Hanrahan' from *Stories of Red Hanrahan* (1897). The title of one of the grades in the Order of the Golden Dawn to which Yeats belonged in the early nineties was Monocris de Astris (Unicorn from the Stars) and it is said in the play that anyone seeing Martin in his frenzy at

the house-burnings might think him apt to hit his head against the
stars. Andrew Hearne also excuses his plan to make everyone
drunk by saying that he is merely lifting them to the stars. In the
end Martin is lifted to the stars through his vision of the unicorns
which implies the completion or perfection of his own spiritual
being. In every case the verbal images are consistent with the
physical presence of the coach ornament and banner. Even the
fire which ends act two and Martin's fiery moment of revelation
are harmonised with the tight pattern of images which replaces
the experimental techniques of music, mime and dance used by
Yeats in other works of this period.

THE PLAYER QUEEN (1922)

Original Publication: Chicago, London and New York, 1922
First Performance: London, 1919

Initially, Yeats conceived of the play as a tragedy and worked at it
for many years, but it did not satisfy him until he rewrote it as a
comedy. *The Player Queen* follows in the footsteps of *The Unicorn
from the Stars*, even to the point of using some of its thematic
material and constructional features. The main idea for the plot is
often traced back to 'The Adoration of the Magi' (1897), which is
reprinted in *Mythologies* (1959) and various interpretations have
been suggested for it. The main action is very simple: the wilful
Decima turns from her poet-husband, whom she loves to torment
and dominate, to take up a new and fulfilling role as queen.
Decima has been a sort of inspiration or ideal to Septimus, but he
has naturally turned for human comfort to Nona and goes off with
her in the end. Decima, on the other hand, exchanges a drunken
poet for a pompous prime minister as she moves from the sphere
of art to that of government. The order of things thus inaugurated
suggests a new dispensation, a contrasting cycle of human
personality and historical development for mankind. Without a
muse Septimus and the older order he represents will surely fall
away from the heights of poetic creation, but we can hardly expect
Decima to become the vehicle and expression of a new
dispensation as the wife of a preposterous prime minister. She
really should be mated with a superhuman beast or bird; but
then, this is a comic presentation and not a serious exposition of

Yeats's philosophical system. Whether there really is a unicorn in the garden, whether Una has copulated with it, or whether Decima now will, is really not very important. All we can be sure of is the fact that the characters and situations are meant to represent a larger scheme of universal order and one which is consistently mocked through comic inversion and deflation.

The great problem with such a plot outline is to identify either reasonable and acceptable motives for the action or a patterned and episodic construction in which the themes of the individual parts repeat and reinforce each other. Yeats divided the play into two formal scenes, allowing the thematically related sequences of the first to establish an ideological frame of reference for the second. Scene one is dominated by Septimus and the burden of the action establishes a comic inversion of exhilaration and poetic ecstasy. Viewed against the desire for peace and sleep expressed by the old men who introduce the scene, Septimus's drunken frenzy is inspired. His state is further emphasised by a contrast with the prosaic platitudes of the older popular poets who have given in to the pettiness and venial nature of social existence. The next episode continues with the idea of degradation and vulgarity as the countrymen and citizens retail the story of the queen copulating with a wild unicorn. Because she does not show herself to her people, the queen's character and motives come into doubt. When we finally see her, we find that she is hardly cut out for acts of bestiality and the unicorn of her imagination is a symbolic beast associated with the ascetic Saint Octima. The so-called political plot or theme of the second scene which involves Una, St Octima, prime minister and commoners is really a dramatic necessity which makes it possible for Decima to exchange roles with the queen. In any case, Una's spirituality and desire to escape from the world is more to the point than the political manoeuvring and it is balanced by Decima's will to dominate and control the world around her. Both women are parodies of the ideal female principle as manifested at opposite points on the great wheel and the unicorn is the image through which they are lifted to a supernatural ecstasy beyond the human condition. The point of Septimus's encounter with the queen's subjects in scene one is both to establish motivation for Decima's assumption of the crown and to further emphasise his own inspired frenzy. Septimus interrupts the intrigue to rant heroically in defence of the unicorn's purity. He is inspired as well as monstrously drunk and gets knocked down for his pains. The final sequence introduces the old beggar who is a grotesque parody of John the Baptist and prophetically announces the accession of each new monarch. Septimus is inevitably linked with the raging old beggar in his role as evangelist for the unicorn and hence the new dispensation which is at hand. What they have in common is inspiration and extranatural power or knowledge which testifies to and substantiates the actual change of roles in the second scene.

When the crucial dialogue between Decima and Nona does take place, its most striking feature is Decima's seemingly calm acceptance of Septimus's defection. Everyone fears her rage and desire for revenge but she only makes a show of looking for a new mate, of fulfilling her need and completing her personality in another way. A conjunction of fate and chance, however, saves her from suicide and enables her to become queen, thereby uniting herself with her own opposite or mask. As Septimus puts it: 'Man is nothing till he is united to an image' (Yeats, 1966, p. 749) and both of them are united to the unicorn, at least imaginatively, as well as to an unsuitable human mate. The play is about love and desire, the love and longing of man for woman, of the natural world for the supernatural, and of all antithetical states of being for each other. The feature which distinguishes this play from Yeats's other work is the fact that the dialectical forces of the universe which divide and unite are seen here as comic and farcical. On-stage the play produces unaffected laughter, but the plot is so elaborately conceived and the characters so numerous and varied that unity and intensity are somewhat sacrificed.

Of course, the consistent use of a neutral and more or less natural prose is a helpful unifying factor in the play and there is a wide enough difference between the petulant speeches of debased characters and the self-mocking inflections of Septimus to provide contrast and variety.

> *First Player.* My God, listen to him! Is it not always the comedian who draws the crowd? Am I dreaming, or was it not I who was called six times before the curtain? Answer me that – (p. 747)

> *Septimus.* You are right. I accept reproach. It is necessary that we who are the last artists – all the rest have gone over to the mob – shall save the images and implements of our art. We must carry into safety the cloak of Noah, the high-crowned

hat of Noah, and the mask of the sister of Noah. She was drowned because she thought her brother was telling lies; certainly we must save her rosy cheeks and rosy mouth, that drowned, wicked mouth. (p. 749)

Greater animation, however, is introduced in the first half of scene two by means of the songs which lead to the climactic dance with the beasts of Noah's ark. The gay and lively sequence of action takes up the middle third of the play and includes four different songs all sung by Decima. The first, '"He went away", my mother sang' (pp. 733 and 734), suggests that the mad singing daughter of a harlot and a drunken sailor might become a great queen because there was a supernatural element in her conception, a seamew cried and a flake of yellow foam dropped upon her mother's thigh. The next two songs, 'Put off that mask of burning gold' and 'O would that I were an old beggar' (pp. 738–9), were also composed by Septimus and have to do with men's tormented longing for the warm embrace of a passionate woman. The last song, 'Shall I fancy beast or fowl?' (p. 744), is closely connected with the dance itself and narrates Decima's search for a suitable lover among the birds and beasts. In it she compares herself to the mythical Pasiphae who fell in love with a sacred bull from the sea and bore it the minotaur, and also to Leda who was raped by Zeus in the form of a swan and gave birth to Helen of Troy. The song offers a second alternative: either Decima will mate with a prince and become a great queen or with a supernatural being in the image of either bird or beast and so give birth to a new age or historical cycle. The dancers, however, are not possessed by godhead and she rejects them, but the visual impact of the cavorting figures costumed as the birds and beasts of Noah's ark is striking and also very comical as a parody of Yeats's usual imagery. The concentrated singing and dancing gives the scene a sense of wild and joyful abandon which is closely related to Septimus's drunken and inspired frenzy in scene one, and contrasts sharply with the more sober and discursive resolution of the action which follows. During the final third of the play Septimus twice sings a two-line refrain which rails against the unicorn's inhuman chastity. The first instance is in heroic and drunken disregard of the approaching mob, the second, as he leaves the betrayed Decima behind. The last fragment of song woven through the action is a two-line refrain taken from the first lyric, which Decima sings after her assumption of the queen's role is confirmed by all present, including the prime minister who is now totally in her power. Decima is actually wearing the queen's robe of state when she sings:

> She pulled the thread, and bit the thread
> And made a golden gown. (p. 758)

Patterns of images, as well as of song, are continued throughout the play and are so organised as to emphasise the essential relationships of characters and action. Instead of lunar references, we find that gold and the sun dominate the play. Much stress, for example, is placed on the tower seen by the light of dawn and the fact that the play within the play is to be performed precisely at noon. The cycle of the moon's twenty-eight phases is here replaced by a solar cycle based on a scale of twenty-four units with women representing noon (objectivity) and mid-night (subjectivity). Decima finds her proper role in life by assuming Una's robe of state and the former queen withdraws to a convent. The other major characters also bear symbolic names which reflect their relationship to one another: Septimus, Octima, and Nona. St Octima, it is said, locked herself up in a tower because a handsome prince was in love with her and Septimus is unfaithful to the ideal woman he worships with Nona who is closer to him on the scale. It may be that the sequence of names is derived from the grade descriptions in the order of the Golden Dawn, an occult study group to which Yeats had belonged, which were based on a dialectical scheme of ten, but their exact meaning is still obscure and private. In any case, Septimus and Octima are imaginative and idealistic archetypes in the play, while Nona and Decima are objective and pragmatic. Octima and Una are inhuman and chaste; concentrating on the one aspect of their natures, they try to escape from the cycle. The unicorn, on the other hand, is complete, being image and beast at one and the same time. Septimus is poet as well as man but giving in to his physical nature, he falls away from his inspiration and turns for comfort to drink and Nona. Decima is both muse and harlot but gives in to her desire for domination and foregoes the possibility of intercourse with the supernatural.

The integration of animal imagery and Christian mythology also helps to underline the point. The unicorn is the symbol of the new dispensation, just as the bull, swan, and donkey refer to earlier historical cycles or periods. Septimus announces the new era and celebrates its image while the old beggar, possessed by the ghost of the played-out Christian annunciation, suggests the end of that dispensation. The dancing animals of Noah's ark and the repeated image of Adam and Eve are also lifeless symbols of an outworn era. Neither the bull-head nor turkey cock are inspired by divinity and god is seen as having played a trick on Adam by creating Eve. The slapstick comedy of Noah, another type of Adam, beating his bad wife, is played off against that of Decima, tormenting and dominating both Septimus and the prime minister. Perhaps the most interesting image and certainly a very significant one, is the mask of Noah's sister which the player queen assumes at the end. A good deal of prominence is given to the device and twice we are told that she was drowned because she did not believe Noah. Decima identifies herself with the mask and acknowledges that she denies the truth of poetry while seeking destruction beside a man about whom she knows nothing. She asks the players to dance by way of ending the play with an image of order and reconciliation, but she also banishes them from her kingdom. On one level, it is a necessary ruse so that her imposture will not be discovered; on another, she banishes subjective creativity and art along with the artists.

The Player Queen is the only one of Yeats's plays not specifically set in Ireland and it was conceived for production on a normal proscenium stage using the movable scenes designed by Edward Gordon Craig as setting. The plain, stylised background and dependence on lighting for mood and tone is eminently suited to so timeless and unreal a sequence of action which unites allegory and fairy tale into an irreverent and amusing spoof of Yeats's philosophy. The use of a play within a play, animal figures, and elaborate costuming, masks, music, dancing, and exaggerated image patterns further distances the material from every-day reality and helps to express its possible meaning.

THE DREAMING OF THE BONES (1919)

Original Publication: Chicago and Dundrum, 1919
First Performance: Dublin, 1931

Because several of Yeats's major themes or ideas are present in *The Dreaming of the Bones*, there has never been much agreement as to the order of their importance, but it is obvious from even the most cursory reflection that they are interdependent. The idea that twentieth century civilisation is on the brink of a new historical cycle to be ushered in by war and violence, for example, is juxtaposed with personal passion and penance experienced by Diarmuid and Dervorgilla who were responsible for the initial step in the progressive political and cultural disintegration of Ireland during the present cycle. The meeting between the ghosts of those long dead and the young man or hero of the play is the symbolic intersection of Ireland's past and her present attempt to free herself from its effects. Rather than the tragic joy of a melting and merging of opposites which offers a release from divided being, the young man has not yet purified himself of his own passionate commitment to a cause and cannot forgive the original treachery of the ghosts. He had fought at the Post Office, that symbol of ultimate resistance and courage, against the British during the Easter Rising of 1916 and is now escaping into hiding. As with most of Yeats's characters, his personality is little developed and about all we learn of him is that he prays sincerely for supernatural protection when alone and is neither a stranger to ghost lore nor a scoffer. He is also sympathetic to the suffering of his fellow man and is moved to forgive the ghostly pair whose story he is told, until he realises that they are, in fact, Diarmuid and Dervorgilla. At this point private and public morality confront one another and public values outweigh everything in the young man's mind. He cannot forgive the guilty pair who are condemned to continue the Dantesque penance which frustrates the passion that brought their treachery into being. On the other hand the young man remains committed to the remorseless hate which will one day free his land, but from which he, in turn, will have to free himself. It is both inevitable and necessary that a modern Cuchulain should be so committed but it is also poignantly sad that the ghosts are not freed from the burden of their remorse. Yeats certainly seems to underline the point by giving the most moving speeches in the play to the ghostly pair when they tell their story in hope of forgiveness.

The third major theme or idea woven through the play is that of the 'dreaming back', one of Yeats's occult doctrines which accounts for the period of spiritual existence between death and rebirth into a new phase on the great wheel. The spirits of the dead expiate the errors of their lives by reliving them until they are purified of the passions which caused them. At that point, they can either be reborn into a new life or, all conditions being perfect, merge into an eternal unity with the supernatural. A good deal of the first half of the play is given over to exposing and explaining the doctrine, and this seems to be as much an end in itself as a necessary justification for the supernatural encounter. The plot has no independent existence or source in traditional mythology and the action is sufficiently bizarre to require substantiation. The central action is derived from an early story, 'Hanrahan's Vision' published in *Stories of Red Hanrahan* (1897), and reprinted in *Mythologies* (1959), in which the ghosts of Diarmuid and Dervorgilla appear to the poet, Hanrahan, in the mist on top of Ben Bulben and seek his forgiveness. But forgiveness is denied them in *The Dreaming of the Bones* as it is in Lady Gregory's *Dervorgilla* (1911) [reprinted in *Collected Plays* 2, 1971] which is another possible source or influence. Forgiveness has no place in the actual doctrine of dreaming back, but is introduced into the play because of the juxtaposition of past and future dispensations. The past must be forgiven in order for the present to fulfil its expectations, but first of all the doctrine of the dreaming back must be fully appreciated, and so it is given prominence in the play.

Nishikigi, A Japanese nōh in which the ghosts of a rejected lover and that of the remorseful woman who ignored his suit are reconciled and released from their attachment to life, was also used as a model but more in the sense of a structural influence than a thematic one. Outside the narrative element which concentrates attention on what has happened to the protagonists in the past and so brings all possible associations with those actions to bear on their present juxtaposition, the most nōh-like characteristic of the play is the travel song (*michi-yuki*) around which Yeats organises the action and the gradual revelation of the mysterious couple's real identity. The composition of the piece follows the pattern which had proved so successful in *At the Hawk's Well* and also in *The Only Jealousy of Emer*, written at about the same time as *The Dreaming of the Bones*. The play opens with a chorus in trimeters which establishes the scene and introduces the main character through a concentration of imagery as well as direct description. The action itself is divided into two parts. The first is expository in terms of the young man's background and the esoteric doctrine which accounts for his encounter with the strange pair. The second half concentrates on the stranger and young girl, relating their past and emphasising the relationship between them and the young man. The whole sequence is ended and its significance confirmed by a choral lyric which parallels the one at the beginning of the play and repeats images introduced there, as well as others from the travel song which marks the division of the action into two distinct parts. The distillation of the action into so limited an interchange is re-echoed by the use of only two verse forms, the very brief and logical trimeters of the songs and the more loosely conceived blank verse of the main characters in which formal iambic pentameters are mixed with irregular lines in accentual verse. Emotional tension is expressed, as usual, by shortening or lengthening the value and number of unstressed syllables as in the young man's speech after refusing his forgiveness and the three characters actually reach the top of the mountain.

> So here we're on the summit. I can see
> The Aran Islands, Connemara Hills,
> And Galway in the breaking light; there too
> The enemy has toppled roof and gable,
> And torn the panelling from ancient rooms;
> What generations of old men had known
> Like their own hands, and children wondered at,
> Has boiled a trooper's porridge. That town had lain,
> But for the pair that you would have me pardon,
> Amid its gables and its battlements
> Like any old admired Italian town.
>
> (Yeats, 1966, pp. 773–4)

The young man is certainly not of the common people. His word-choice, syntax, and frame of reference identify him more closely with an objective intellectual or principle of the mind, which indeed he is as well as being a flesh-and-blood revolutionary, a modern Adam or Cuchulain. Likewise, the choral lyrics are refined and depersonalised in register as well as somewhat stylised by the use of interlocking rhyme in the opening choruses, the travel song, and the two lyrics which end the piece. The musical effect is very successful in performance as the rhymes ring sharply in such short lines, and especially so when sung.

The effect of the rhythmic interplay thus achieved further emphasises a pattern of images which is directly associated with the meaning of the action. The first song, 'Why does my heart beat so' (pp. 762–3), expresses fear at the thought of an encounter with a supernatural apparition, an image projected by the spirits of the dead. Dreams spring from the dry bones of the dead, and because of the intense passion of the dreamers the valley is often filled to overflowing with them like a jade or agate cup overfilled with wine. The reference to dry bones brings in associations of prophetic vision as in Ezekiel 37. 1–14 and the images or dreams so generated are then associated with the spiritual as well as physical intoxication of wine in an exotic stone cup. The exaltation or ecstasy of the dreams is a refined and precious experience which is characterised by the elevation of nature (mountain valley and human passion) to the level of an artifact (jade cup filled with wine). The logical development from the respectively violent and drunken visions of Martin Hearne in *The Unicorn from the Stars* or those of Septimus in *The Player Queen* are fairly obvious. The same images are repeated in the speeches which follow and are further sustained by elaboration of context and association with parallel figures. The travel song, 'Why should the heart take fright?' (pp. 767–8), picks up the imagery of the human heart and the visions projected by dry bones, but combines them with two other elements or patterns of images, each of which represents one of the major themes of the play. The three stanzas in blank verse spoken by the first musician describe the journey up the mountain in terms of symbolic landscape. The first stage is symbolised by a fouled well with an owl crying overhead, past which mourners carry the dead for burial. The scene can be taken as an image of temporal existence and its transiency. The second round brings the climbers to death itself; past grassy fields, ragged thorns and a gap in the hedge to where the owls are nested in the tombs at their feet. The third shows them above the manifestations of both mutable nature and the cat-headed owl of death or supernatural knowledge, in a world of unchanging stone.

The songs parallel a similar progression in terms of human reaction to life and death. Each stanza, however, is divided into an assertion of four lines and a related refrain which serves all three. In the first the singer asks why should the heart take fright, it is only the night which makes man lonely and afraid. The second contrasts head and heart; objectively, the singer is ready to sacrifice life (young rebel) but subjectively, he is attached to the passion of life by memory (Diarmuid and Dervorgilla). In the third, the night-time dreams of the dry bones prevail and because there is no light at all, neither moon nor sun, calamity can have its fling. In terms of the dialectic processes of universal order, it is the moment between two cycles and the refrain calls out for the annunciation of a new order. The red cock of March is the universal harbinger of a new dawn as well as being a ready symbol of sexuality and combat. The red cock of March must be especially potent and violent as it is associated with spring and the regeneration of nature. In historical terms the red cock is associated with the spiritual cycle of Christ's death and rebirth, and, in a previous cycle, with that of Mars, god of war. Should the new cycle be announced, the moment of exposure, of subjective anarchy, would be over. In the lyric which ends the play, 'At the grey round of the hill' (pp. 775– 6), we find just that to be the case. The wild music of the night wind and of the dreaming bones which captures man's mind and withers his chance to control his life actively, is stilled. The second of the two lyrics which make up the section repeats the pattern of the entire play by stating that the singer's heart had run wild at the cry of gull and owl, but now the new dawn has come and he is safe, he has heard the cock crow. However distilled and difficult the songs may be, they do offer a consistent and coherent statement of Yeats's themes.

Images from the main body of the play also complement the tight pattern within the songs and in at least one instance have the added force of physical representation on stage. When the strangers enter, the lantern carried by the hero is blown out, plunging him into total darkness in that hour before dawn when even the moon is covered up, a darkness which represents the moment of anarchy between cycles. All the other imagery, however, is verbal rather than being represented physically on stage, and the most significant cluster in the play centres on either the loneliness of the bird cries or the Abbey of Corcomroe. The birds who cry in their loneliness at the beginning of the play later merge with the owl of the travel song and combine with the curlew (gull) and cat-headed bird (owl) at the end. All are figures of subjective, introspective personalities.

The abbey on the other hand, is specifically associated with the more objective and active control of life through the story of Donough O'Brien who died nearby in the fourteenth century after an abortive insurrection. The party to which he belonged had enlisted Scottish aid in their struggle against the King of Thomend in much the same way that Diarmuid and Dervorgilla had sought to ally themselves with Henry II of England in the twelfth century. O'Brien's story serves as a point of comparison and contrast by which to emphasise the enormity of Diarmuid's treachery. The locale of the abbey is an excellent choice as it is a natural scene for an escape to the Aran Isles by a Dublin rebel. The associations of the ruined abbey, its graveyard, and the mountain path which winds up the sides of the cup-like stone valley merge with the idea of age-old political violence that has unroofed Ireland and despoiled its ancient heritage. The white paths themselves which are explicitly called to mind at the opening of the play and the circuits of the stage made by the main characters which give theatrical reality to the journey described by the travel song, are meant to suggest the winding and unwinding of the passionate thread of a prior existence. By contrast with O'Brien's political manoeuvres, the love story of Diarmuid and Dervorgilla has the intensity and dimensions of myth, while the physical climb up the mountain brings the main characters to a symbolic point at which that story can be retold as objectively and sympathetically as possible. The pause for rest in their ascent permits the narrative of past events and the imagery of the travel song introduces a further level of meaning. The real climax of the play, however, is in the refusal which follows, while the final circuit of the stage and dance of unrequited love provides a resolution for the piece. The lovers cannot be forgiven, however poignant their plight, and the cycles of necessity must progress in their normal way. The lonely birds and unroofed monument as they are defined by symbolic stage movement and the imagery of the songs, determine rather than reflect character and condition.

Music is another important device in the play and the combination of drum, zither, and flute marking the final circuit of the stage, the last turn of the old dispensation after the young man has denied his forgiveness, is a striking feature of the play's production method. The climax is reached as much in terms of sound and sight as it is in terms of the construction and meaning of the literary text. *The Dreaming of the Bones* is conceived of as a dance drama and the poignancy of the lovers' plight is expressed directly through their dances. The impossibility of forgiveness is seen in the intransigence of the hero before whose solitary and unbending figure they dance. As in all the dance plays, the general idea is to suggest circumstances and emotions before acting them out and many distancing devices are called into play to achieve this end. In addition to music and dance, masks are used for the stranger and young girl, presumably to help the audience to see them as spirits or images rather than real people. In the same way the musicians are made up to look as though masked since they too are principles of the mind, intermediators between the real world and the world of ideas represented by the characters and situations. They appear in the actual world of the audience, in a normal room or studio and not on a conventional stage, while exposition is accomplished during the ritual folding and unfolding of a decorated cloth through the imagery of choral narration and commentary.

The dance is another, and perhaps the most striking, of the extra-literary devices used in the play. From the narration we deduce that it is highly mimetic; they gaze passionately at one another, turn away and cover their eyes. Yeats may have had a stylised gesture from the Japanese nōh in mind which indicates uncontrollable weeping and the deepest sorrow, but the only requirement of the dancer is to express the emotional quality of frustrated longing. The dance also takes on deeper overtones of significance in the context of the young hero's running commentary on the destruction and degradation that the lovers brought to Ireland. On repeating his refusal to forgive them the intersection of historical cones or gyres is again emphasised by the purgatorial vision of the lovers expiating the past in the presence of the young man who unconsciously heralds the emergence of a new and antithetical age.

CALVARY (1920)

Original Publication: London and New York, 1921
First Performance: ——

A play which takes Christ for its hero is not so radical a departure from Yeats's perennial themes as it might appear, particularly when one notes just how heretical a view of Christ's crucifixion this play presents. One of the major sources for the play is Oscar Wilde's 'The Doer of Good' (1894) [reprinted in *Works*, 1948] and the theme was first formulated by the hero of Yeats's early short story, 'The Tables of the Law' (1897) which is reprinted in *Mythologies* (1959): 'I am not among those for whom Christ died, and this is why I must be hidden. I have a leprosy that even eternity cannot cure. I have seen the whole, and how can I come again to believe that a part is the whole? I have lost my soul because I have looked out of the eyes of the angels.' (Yeats, 1959, pp. 305–6) Yeats's idea is not incompatible with Christianity but it is certainly unorthodox.

He held that the individual should rely upon and develop the Christ-like will and imagination within one rather than depend on the external and objective intervention of a Christ figure. Everyone can and should realise the potential of Christ, an archetypal and subjective human being reaching out to complete his nature by merging with the perfectly objective divinity inherent in his being. Christ and Cuchulain are related figures, but Cuchulain dies as an antithetical objective hero and fulfils himself or completes his being by merging with a subjective ideal. According to tradition both Christ and Cuchulain combine temporal and divine natures as they are both born of human mothers and fathered by supernatural agencies. In *Calvary* Yeats examines the development of the human Christ as he progresses symbolically through the last phases of his life cycle towards union with his own opposite. His progress is measured by a series of confrontations with other characters whose needs and natures reflect aspects of his own. Lazarus is the first to appear, but instead of gratitude for being brought back to life, he claims Christ's approaching death for himself. Here, Lazarus is an example of phase twenty-seven on the great wheel, the phase of the saint, which is characterised by renunciation and passivity. He chooses the oblivion and wholeness of death over the suffering and incompleteness of life in the body. His longing is shared by Christ who also reflects the phase of the saint in allowing past experience to flow in upon himself and express itself through his acts and thoughts. Like Lazarus, Christ begins to perceive the true source of his total life and acknowledges the need for penance. Christ contends that he is not wholly responsible since he does his father's will, but Lazarus retorts: 'And not your own'. (Yeats, 1966, p. 783)

The first musician's description of Martha and the three Marys who break in upon the scene and can exist only through Christ's redeeming love, introduces a sharp contrast at this point. We are reminded that not everyone refuses Christ's intervention in the temporal world and for such as these his external existence and providence justifies their lives. The scene of Christ's faithful followers embracing him and wiping his blood-stained feet with their hair is conjured up in imagination, but not physically presented as is the previous encounter. The intervention serves a dramatic purpose rather than a symbolic one and marks the division between the first two encounters by providing a relevant contrast. Christ's followers flee as Judas approaches for he is as antithetical to them as they are to Lazarus. Judas is an example of the hunchback, an image of the twenty-sixth phase of the great wheel, which in fact precedes that of the saint. He represents the beginnings of self-realisation, the desire to understand experience rationally and to judge it objectively. Judas betrays Christ in order to create his own personality. He admits to challenging Christ's power, knowing that He is god and that the act of betrayal is predestined but he rivals god's power in so far as a man can by taking upon himself the responsibility for choosing to fulfil god's plan. Judas' choice amounts to a kind of existential act of the spirit or will. It places him outside Christ's active pity for the limitations of the human condition, just as Lazarus remains outside that divine pity through his renunciation of life. Judas' victory is acknowledged when Christ vainly attempts to dismiss him. The three Roman soldiers interrupt the action and Judas remains on stage to hold up the cross against which Christ stretches out his arms. Having chosen to sacrifice himself, Christ now assumes the same role of passivity and renunciation of the body that Lazarus had earlier dramatised.

The Roman soldiers, in their turn, represent the last and final human type, the fool of the twenty-eighth and final phase of human development in any lifetime. They represent Christ's anti-self or mask in that phase, the opposite which the hero must become in order to achieve the much-desired oblivion. The soldiers have no aspirations and ask nothing of their god. They are not interested in making a god-like choice, but are content with chance. Whatever happens is acceptable, and as gamblers, they know that eventually a balance is struck between winning and losing. They not only negate Christ's sacrifice but also add irony by imagining that their independence of the crucified god must be a comfort to him. Christ's reaction is typical of phase twenty-eight; he is overcome by fear and envy of effective and intelligent actions. As they mime a quarrel and reconciliation while dancing around the cross, Christ cries out in despair: 'My Father, why hast Thou forsaken Me.' (p. 787) The play is not so much concerned with the dual nature of Christ and the doctrine of the resurrection as it is about the limitations of orthodox Christianity and its place in a larger scheme of universal forces and personality types. Christ's active pity for man's common lot leads him to Calvary and his suffering lies in the realisation that his divine pity does not reach everyman. Christ does not die for Lazarus, Judas, or the Roman soldiers, but ultimately for himself. His encounters with them represent the final stages of his development towards that death.

In so short and tightly constructed a play the conception of the action as a dream or vision projected by the passionate mind of the dead Christ is an important feature. The action is thus removed from direct association with the truth of either historical fact or orthodox tradition. The subjective reality of Christ's passion as reinterpreted by Yeats is the real subject of the piece and the doctrine of dreaming back justifies the representation. The intensity of the experience causes the limitations of the sacrifice and Christ's exposure to public mockery to be relived in imagination over and over again.

The first musician's opening speech and song set the pattern by repeated reference to the mockers who instil a frenzied fear in his heart, their cries being compared to the playing of a flute made from the thigh bone of a moon-crazed heron. The elaborate image is central to the meaning of the play and forms part of an extended pattern of references to solitary birds and especially to waterfowl. Bird imagery generally expresses an ideal of perfect subjectivity and self-sufficient introspection while the thigh bone of a moon-crazed waterfowl suggests the ambiguities of sexuality and mutability which pure spirit experiences in the temporal world. The music of such a flute is as much a mockery as the cries of objective personalities who do not participate in Christ's sacrifice. The antithetical image which represents the extreme objective position is the dice carved from an old sheep's thigh bone which are associated with the Roman soldiers. The opposed symbolism of bird and beast is common enough in Yeats's work but in this play the emphatic pattern of imagery is almost entirely centred on birds. Lazarus is said to go out to the desert places among solitary birds, and deprived of Christ's love, the three Marys are compared to birds' feathers tossed on the bitter sea under a full moon. Even Judas is associated with a bird when he mentions that he planned to betray Christ in the presence of a solitary heron. The opening and closing songs help to establish the main point of the play through imagery alone. The heron of the first song does not prey upon the leaping fish but rather contemplates its own image in the water under the full moon. The refrain of the closing song reiterates the idea but specifies gull, eagle, and swan as different character types whose fulfilment is found only in the context of their own natures and qualities. The juxtaposition of moon and bird imagery with Christ's crucifixion repeats and re-emphasises the idea that individuals must work out their own salvation. The play itself reveals a larger pattern of universal order by presenting Christ's ritual participation in its cycle.

In keeping with the general development of Yeats's dramatic form, *Calvary* depends as much on musical or rhythmic composition as it does on esoteric philosophy and symbolic character relationships. Three distinct verse forms are employed; iambic pentameter for dramatic dialogue, tetrameters for the opening and closing songs, 'Motionless under the moon-beam' (pp. 780–1) and 'Lonely the sea-bird lies at her rest' (pp. 787–8), and trimeters for the two intense lyrics which mark the beginnings of the first and second encounters, 'O, but the mockers' cry' (pp. 781–2) and 'Take but His love away.' (p. 784) There is little variation of line length within the individual speeches while the syntax and vocabulary are more colloquial, direct, and modern than ever. An occasional archaism or slightly stylised turn of phrase does elevate the language from time to time and helps to characterise it as heroic.

> *Judas.* That was the very thought that drove me wild.
> I could not bear to think you had but to whistle
> And I must do; but after that I thought,
> 'Whatever man betrays Him will be free.' (pp. 784–5)

> *First Musician.*
> But where have last year's cygnets gone?
> The lake is empty; why do they fling

White wing out beside white wing?
What can a swan need but a swan? (p. 788)

First Musician.
  Take but His love away,
  Their love becomes a feather
  Of eagle, swan or gull,
  Or a drowned heron's feather
  Tossed hither and thither
  Upon the bitter spray
  And the moon at the full. (p. 784)

The use of rhyme in the songs further emphasises their musical intensity and causes them to contrast all the more sharply with the heroic dialogue. At the same time the distinction between the ballad-like stanzas in tetrameters and the more emotionally charged lyrics in trimeters creates an atmosphere of heightened mystery and strangeness which throws the main action into even greater prominence. The subtle interplay of verse rhythms is not insisted upon throughout, however, and instead of being repeated at the end of the encounter with Judas or that with the soldiers, a symbolic stage picture and dance are substituted.

It would be difficult to represent the raising of Lazarus visually but the dialogue establishes the image of his cloth-wrapped body and tomb. The physical presence of the three Marys and Christ's followers is also avoided in favour of description and evocation by verbal imagery. As tension mounts to a climax, however, and Judas confronts Christ directly, words give way to action. Judas holds up the cross while Christ stretches out his arms against it through the rest of the play. That traditional image is especially powerful in so unorthodox a sequence of action and it takes on new dimensions as the Roman soldiers circle the immobilised pair in a dance, miming the throwing of dice which resolves their symbolic quarrel. In both cases a visual representation of their actual natures, aspirations and relationships reinforces the implicit theme of the text. The dramatic conflict is both presented verbally and acted out in a series of contrasting encounters which ends with Christ's helpless despair over the inevitable inadequacy of his sacrifice.

Like *The Dreaming of the Bones* and the other plays for dancers, *Calvary* owes something to the influence of the Japanese nōh, but the combination and weighting of theatrical elements Yeats employs is certainly unique and original. It has been argued that the Pound-Fenollosa version of *Kakitsubata* might have served as a structural model. In that play a flower spirit first assumes the appearance of a local girl who recounts the attachment of Narihira, a classical poet and patron of art, to a place famous for its water iris. She then appears as a great lady, Narihira's lover, and finally as the spirit of flowers, miming his presence through her dancing and also the passing of a golden age. Whether or not the influence of this particular play can be proved, there is certainly a good deal of general assimilation of nōh technique in *Calvary* as in each of the other dance plays. The use of a privileged and ritualised narration which is structured around a central verbal image or cluster of images and also expressed by a combination of stage picture, mime or dance, musical accompaniment and song was at least confirmed if not inspired by classical Japanese theatre. The limitation of action to the recreation in imagination of a passionate moment of experience and the use of masks to emphasise the archetypal or representative nature of the characters can also be traced to Yeats's interest in nōh. The ceremonial folding and unfolding of the cloth which underlines the function of the chorus as mediators between the real world of the audience and the symbolic actions of the players is original, however, as is the removal of the dramatic action from the theatre in order to break down the conventional assumptions and responses of audiences to dramatic representation. In fact all the dance plays rely on performance techniques almost as heavily as on the quality of the literary texts for their effects.

THE CAT AND THE MOON (1926)

Original Publication: London, Chicago, and Dublin, 1924
First Performance: Dublin, 1931

Although published much later, *The Cat and the Moon* was written in 1917. The play was conceived as a comic interlude to be performed between serious dramas in much the same way that Japanese kyogen relieve the severity of a nōh programme by introducing an antithetical mood and subject matter. Yeats knew very little about kyogen and instead of imitating its character and content, he wrote a farce in much the same form he had developed for the serious dance plays. *The Cat and the Moon* does incorporate some characteristics of nōh as well as those of kyogen including a travel song after which the journey is suggested by a circuit of the playing area. An actual place is celebrated, St Colman's Well, just a few miles from Yeats's house in Galway. Other features common to the nōh form are also included, such as the use of chorus, musicians, masks, a unifying image pattern, supernatural apparitions, the restriction of action to a passionate moment and a climactic dance. There was a single kyogen translation among the Fenollosa papers which Yeats had studied, *Kikazu Zato*, in which a blind man and a deaf man play tricks on one another based upon their infirmities. The central action of *The Cat and the Moon* cannot be said to derive solely from the Japanese source, however. It is also closely related to J. M. Synge's *The Well of the Saints* (1905) [reprinted in *Collected Works*, 1962] and, of course, to its source, *Moralité de l'aveugle et du boiteux* by André de La Vigne.

In the French version the afflicted pair are cured by sacred relics carried in a passing procession. The blind man is delighted but the lame man curses the saint who has worked the miracle because he has put an end to the beggar's easy life. Synge, on the other hand, gives us a pair of blind beggars, Martin and Mary Doul, whose miraculous cure results in a sharp contrast between their former life of simple charity coupled with subjective reality and their present descent into the corrupting and sordid objective reality of a petty bourgeois society. The play ends with a refusal to have their sight restored a second time and the voluntary resumption of a happier and more imaginative life. In Yeats's reworking of the theme the blind beggar chooses his sight and active control over the physical world while the lame beggar chooses to be blessed and enters into a life of the spirit which transcends human limitations. Within the context of the action the two beggars are easily identified as symbolic deformities of body (blindness) and mind or soul (lameness). Respectively, they represent objective and subjective principles in search of wholeness or self-fulfilment. The effort Yeats made in notes and prefaces to associate the figures with Irish legend and St Colman's Well in particular, is strangely inconclusive, however. He claimed to have forgotten the story except for the fact that a lame man on a blind man's back sought and found a well which cured them (see

Jeffares, 1975, pp. 173 and 4). There is a similar incident recorded by Lady Gregory in *Cuchulain of Muirthemne*. According to the legend of 'Cruachan', Nera, who had entered the hill of the sidhe, saw a blind man with a lame man upon his back making his way each day to a well to see if the king's crown were still safely hidden there. On asking why they rather than anyone else should be given the task, he was told that the king himself had blinded the one and lamed the other. In *The Cat and the Moon* the beggars not only find the holy well but also gain access to its miraculous powers and in their different ways complete or perfect themselves. One becomes physically whole, the other spiritually enlightened.

The comic aspects of the play are not so pronounced and uproarious as those of either *The Green Helmet* or *The Player Queen*, for example. A good deal of serious exposition and substantiation of philosophical doctrine is present. In establishing the symbolic characters and situations, for instance, the interdependency of body and mind or soul is insisted upon while the distinction between the blind and lame beggar is underlined by the association of the lame man with flightiness of mind. One recalls the opposition of blind man (Cuchulain) and fool (Conchubar) in *On Baile's Strand*. The dialogue between the two beggars raises the question of their actual relationship with the saint. Saints and sinners are also interdependent according to the text and this relationship accounts for the interpolated analogy satirising Edward Martin as the holy man of Laban and George Moore as the old lecher. The saint is no more complete or self-sufficient than the beggars. He interrupts their dialogue at exactly the mid-point of the play to confess his loneliness, asking first one and then the other to abide with him always. Up to this point there has not been much comedy, except for the anti-heroic conception of deformed beggars as heroes and the parody of Yeat's theory of historical cycles in the thousand-odd steps they count out to find the well. In the second half of the play, however, the restoration of the blind beggar's vision confirms his suspicion that the lame man has stolen his black sheepskin and the sequence ends with a ritualised drubbing mimed as a dance. The comic inversion of the now-blessed beggar being beaten for his sins is a vivid image of life's ambiguities, but it is followed by another and more serious symbol of universal order. The saint who is as invisible to the unregenerated audience as to the blind beggar is said to mount the lame man's back, commanding him to dance. In the same way that mind or soul (lame beggar) had ridden body (blind beggar) at the beginning of the play, the saint now rides on the back of the lame beggar. A new dispensation or epoch is announced which must be seen as an even greater miracle than the cure of bodily deformity. Emphasis and importance is given to the fact by making the still-deformed beggar dance. Instead of a solemn ritual of benediction with the lame man making a formal obeisance to the cardinal points of the compass, he is urged on to a wild dance, presumably carrying the saint on his back until his exit. The working out of the action (the lyrical structure of the play) is thus very similar to that of all the other dance plays. After a choral introduction the exposition and rising action is established in a series of brief episodes which lead to a medial climax or intervention and on to a resolution expressed through dance and a choral commentary or closing. The scheme is effective, even with the slight subject matter of *The Cat and the Moon*.

The gentle comedy of the play is certainly underlined and substantiated by the prose style which is a lively version of the familiar peasant dialect Yeats uses from the beginning of his career. Rhythmically, the speeches are cast in short sense units of similar lengths and stress patterns, while a larger number of inversion and Gaelic locutions than usual are employed. In this way, the musical effect of verse is strongly suggested.

> *Lame Beggar.* Because there's no one to see a man slipping in at the door, or throwing a leg over the wall of a yard, you are a bitter temptation to many a poor man, and I say it's not right, it's not right at all. There are poor men that because you are blind will be delayed in Purgatory.
>
> (Yeats, 1966, p. 795)

In addition to the lyrical effect of the dialogue, the beggars use such vividly concrete images and imaginative figures that the result is highly poetic and spontaneously joyful.

> *Lame Beggar.* Haven't I been telling you from the peep o' day that my sheepskin is that white it would dazzle you?
> *Blind Beggar.* Are you so swept with the words that you've never thought that when I had my own two eyes, I'd see what colour was on it? (p. 801)

By comparison the saint speaks prosaically, in brief sentences without a repeating rhythm, and blandly, without either decorative syntax or figures. On the other hand, his speeches are given by the first musician as a choral intervention and they are inevitably associated with the highly charged and mysterious imagery of the songs which are delivered by the same voice.

The exact relationship of cat and moon to the blind beggar and lame man is perhaps not so far-fetched as it appears at first, even though there is little or no explicit association of the one pair with the other in the actual text of the play. The title of the play is about the only piece of evidence that the cat and moon somehow characterise or represent the action of the whole as well as provide the imagery for the opening, travel and closing songs. Minnaloushe, at any rate, is a real cat and not a cat-headed man or bird as in *The Green Helmet* or *The Dreaming of the Bones*. It is an objective animal (beast not bird) which responds to the progressive phases of the subjective moon by reflecting the changes in the shape-changing pupils of its eyes. The comparison is perhaps extravagant but if we project it into the main action of the play, we can easily associate the beggars with cats as they respond to the saint who represents those supernatural forces which govern the temporal world. The objective body (blind man) rejects the beatific vision and is cured of its deformity while the subjective human mind (lame man) joins its closest kin, the saint, and enters into a new phase of spiritual being. Even without Yeats's helpful notes we could work out the relationships from the songs themselves and our prior experience of his basic symbols. In the opening lyric, 'The cat went here and there' (pp. 792–3), the creeping black cat is both nearest kin and antithesis to the revolving white moon which obviously governs it and troubles its animal blood. The travel song, 'Minnaloushe runs in the grass' (p. 794) insists on the delicate dance the moon induces in the cat and foreshadows the lame man's dance at the end of the play when he unites with his nearest kin, the saint. A new dispensation is inaugurated and the force which governs the universe changes its nature at the same time and learns a new dance. The closing song seems to propose a general application of the theory of cycles. The moon is now sacred. Minnaloushe, who creeps about in its light, is as unaware of its direct influence on his life and as immersed in his own self-importance as the rest of us. All sublunary creatures follow the moon through each character phase as inevitably and unselfconsciously as the pupils of the cat's eyes reflect its waxing and waning.

> Minnaloushe creeps through the grass
> Alone, important and wise,
> And lifts to the changing moon
> His changing eyes. (p. 804)

The subjective soul is said to recognise its separate being at the full of the moon, its absorption in god at the dark.

Unlike the dances, the songs are not related to visual stage images, except for the travel song derived from nõh which is here accompanied by a ritual circling of the stage to indicate the beggar's journey to the holy well. The grotesque masks are certainly a strong visual reminder of the action's representative nature. They imply that the characters are principles of the mind rather than real human beings, while the only visual indication of the setting is a patterned screen or curtain suggesting St Colman's Well. The verbal references to the scene give a picture of ash trees above and a flat stone beside the wall which may or may not be represented visually. For an audience familiar with Yeats's plays the site is inevitably associated with the well and trees of *At the Hawk's Well*. Comparisons and contrasts abound. *The Cat and the Moon* insists on a comic inversion of heroic, antique, and Celtic archetypes which are now incorporated into an anti-heroic, contemporary and Christian farce. The beggars, however, are granted their desire by the saint while Cuchulain is frustrated in his purpose by the woman of the sidhe.

Movement and music, more than stage pictures, serve to underline the action of *The Cat and the Moon*. The mimed journey and dances are especially important, and the ritual folding and unfolding of the cloth during the opening and closing songs is only omitted for practical reasons. Since the play is meant as a comic interlude between serious dance plays, the musicians need not be reintroduced as they would already be on stage. The entrance of the beggar, one on the back of the other, is a strong visual statement of their relationship and the idea is further reinforced by the simulation of the journey with the lame beggar again being carried by the blind man. The two dances, however, express the wider implications of the action, the antagonism or opposition of body and mind within the forced interdependency of their co-existence in man and the joy experienced at their release from one another. The blind beggar mimes a comic drubbing of the lame man who has been caught out in his deceptions. The lame beggar's dance with the saint upon his back is the miraculous image of his admission into spiritual experience and herald of a new cycle with different qualities or characteristics from the one which preceded it. Yeats seemed to have satisfied himself as to exactly how the lame beggar should move; at least he specifies that the movements should be either formal and stiff as those of a puppet or highly stylised as in a dance. In every way, vulgar realism or direct imitation of every-day life is avoided, even in a kyogen-like farce. The representational aspect of characters and actions are stongly emphasised and re-emphasised. Not only the expressive dance of the main characters but also every movement of the lame beggar is artfully stylised. The dances themselves are further heightened by the accompaniment of appropriate music; drums and flute for the beating of the lame man by the blind beggar, cymbals clashing for the miraculous dance of the lame man with the saint upon his back.

4   Late Plays

THE RESURRECTION (1931)

Original Publication: London and Dublin, 1931
First Performance: Dublin, 1934

Like *Calvary* which is an overtly heretical reinterpretation of
Christian mythology, Yeats realised that the subject matter of *The
Resurrection* made it unsuitable for the public stage in England and
Ireland. The form developed for the earlier dance plays proved a
very practical vehicle for the material and permitted it to be
produced effectively for a small audience of initiates outside a
conventional theatre. The main action presents the revelation of
man's divinity in the near orthodox story of Christ's miraculous
resurrection from the dead and provides a mirror image or mask
of the death of Christ in *Calvary* as a projection of god's humanity.
There is something more to the play, however, than a mere
retelling of the gospel story. The parallel imagery of Dionysian
death and resurrection which is found in the songs of the
musicians and echoed by the minor action of unseen worshippers
in the streets, emphasises the relationship of Christ's resurrection
to a cyclical view of history and human personality which is
explicitly associated with a Heraclitian doctrine of flux.

The characters are as nameless and representative as any in
Yeats's mature plays. They are principles of the mind who exhibit
characteristic responses to Christ's nature as both man and god,
while expressing and explaining the world-view which informs
that reaction. The Hebrew believes that Christ is merely a man
and must die a conventional, human death. The Greek, on the
other hand, believes that Christ is nothing less than a god and,
being supernatural, cannot die. The opposition of their positions
provides the major conflict of the play and its resolution is
foreshadowed by the Syrian who is ready to accept an unnatural

synthesis of their different views. He alone is willing to admit the possibility of irrationality and the beginning of a new cycle or dispensation. Unlike the others the Syrian is ready to allow the possibility of a new and miraculous category, a man/god who dies and does not die, who experiences death as a man but overcomes death as a god and still retains a human body of flesh and blood. The validity of the three characters is carefully established in the play through detailed and accurate references to actions and situations as recorded in the gospels. Because the historical account of the crucifixion is very real for European and American audiences, the fictional Hebrew, Greek, and Syrian who attend the apostles on the third day also assume a measure of that reality. Close reference to the biblical account of Christ's appearance to his apostles is also used to close the play and to reinforce the sense of miracle and mystery in the Greek's troubled recognition of the dual nature of Christ as both god and man.

The dialogue between the Hebrew and the Greek is interrupted by the appearance of the worshippers of Dionysus in the street outside and by their song which marks a turning point in the progress of the play. In the first half the main characters discuss their different views of Christ and their most considered statements occur just before and after the intervention of the dancers and their song. The Hebrew recognises the need to deny or obliterate the individual will in order that deity take complete possession and divine suffering descend into man's soul, making it pure. He is glad that Christ has died and is proven to be a mere man for he would otherwise have tried to follow that impossible example. On discovering the truth too late, he might have ended in bitter remorse for the normal life he would have sacrificed. The Alexandrian Greek, whose culture is an extension and debasement of classical conventions, states his own world-view in response to the worshippers of Dionysus who have abandoned themselves to an ecstasy of emotion and physical debauch. They deny the self in the sense of abandoning reason or self-control, which is the opposite of the unnaturalness and asceticism of the Hebrew's self-denial. The Greek compares the present self-surrender and self-debasement of Dionysian worship with the classical concept of deity in which gods and goddesses are not indifferent to human fate, but do not interfere with man's soul. In this view the gods are eternally self-contained and do not need to possess men. They are, however, accessible through contemplation and they exhibit a high, keen joy in their perfect mastery and control of the universe. Heroic men and women may also possess that joy by copying divine gestures and acts. They are the only humans admired by the gods, and they remain separate, retaining their own souls. The conflicting views coincide with the characteristic relationship of subjective and objective personalities to the supernatural which we have encountered over and over again in the middle plays. The Hebrew represents man's encounter with the supernatural as a suspension of selfhood and denial of the physical body which results in the absorption of the individual into a spiritual state. The Greek sees it as a close parallelism of high heroism and joyfully disinterested action which raises man to the nature and quality of the gods without sacrificing separateness or individuality. As the action of the play progresses from that ideological watershed, however, it becomes apparent that the opposed views are being set up in order to be denied, or, at best, superseded.

The Syrian enters immediately after the Greek's speech and dialogue commences, leading eventually to the dramatic revelation of Christ's actual nature as both god and man, spiritual and physical, subjective and objective. As it turns out, deity is neither a phantom possessing a human body nor heroic man imitating the gestures and actions of a god, but rather a spiritual being who overcomes the ultimate limitation of man's mortality and yet exists as a creature of flesh and blood. The supreme mystery is a phantom with a beating heart.

The point at which the philosophical positions of Hebrew and Greek intersect is the image of Dionysus and related allusions which assume great structural importance in the play. The figure of Dionysus is central to the opening, medial, and closing songs as well as being the immediate subject of the repeated description of off-stage dances at the middle and end of the drama. Traditionally a god of subjective passion and ecstasy, Dionysus was begotten by Zeus on Persephone, a mortal woman, and when he was torn to pieces by Titans, Pallas Athene, the virgin goddess, snatched up his heart and carried it to his father who swallowed it and begot him a second time upon Semele, another mortal woman. The associations with Christ are numerous; both are products of intercourse between the natural and supernatural worlds and each is a type of regeneration or nature god who overcomes death and is miraculously born again. In terms of the play's imagery the virginity of Athene is an important link between the two myths as is Yeats's use of the beating heart which confirms the miraculous revelation of Christ's resurrection. The worship of Dionysus is a form of mystery religion which Yeats sees as the mask or antiself of the classical concept of objective and heroic archetypes. He follows the dialectical argument of Friedrich Nietzsche in *The Birth of Tragedy* (1872, translated 1909) who suggested that the opposition between the principle of reason (Apollo) and passion (Dionysus) found its proper expression in terms of tragic conflict. The description of the dancing worshippers emphasises the abandon and passionate licence of their world-view. They are transvestites carrying an image of the dead god and seeking ecstasy in total submission to him. Some engage in flagellation, others copulate shamelessly in the street, and they then go off, expressing their grief and longing for the return of their god in terms of a desire for sexual intercourse. On their return at the end of the play they sing joyously that their god has risen, but wait expectantly, staring at the house in which Christ is about to appear. Instead of Dionysus being reborn, a new god has been resurrected, an archetype whose divine objectivity is exactly equal to his human subjectivity. Christ is not just a god reborn, but a new god whose nature will characterise the succeeding age.

The three songs confirm the importance of Dionysus to the main theme of the play. The first, 'I saw a staring virgin stand' (Yeats, 1966, p. 903), outlines the central action of the regeneration myth and emphasises the idea of recurring cycles as ritual representations, either of the natural year or larger units of one thousand years (*magnus annus*).

> And then did all the Muses sing
> Of Magnus Annus at the Spring,
> As though God's death were but a play. (p. 903)

In a new cycle we cannot expect a replay of similar events until all phases of its course are run through. In terms of the song the rise and fall of Troy are paralleled by that of Rome when the Virgin Mary and Christ made their prophetic appearance on the scene. The fierce virgin and her star actually refer to an image in Virgil's Fourth Eclogue which alludes to Astrea, daughter of Zeus, goddess of justice and protector of men in the golden age, who was transformed into the constellation Virgo, carrying the star Spica in her hand. Traditionally, however, the image has been interpreted by Christian commentators as a prophecy of Christ's birth. The song makes the same point as the play. The cycle might be expected to repeat itself; Astrea and Spica (justice) being to the age which began with the Roman empire what Athene and Dionysus are to that which began with the fall of Troy. In this case, however, Mary and Christ are substituted. The second song, 'Astrea's holy child!' (p. 917), again mixes the Astrea myth with that of Dionysus. The principle of justice dies the death of Dionysus and is invoked by the women in terms of sexual fulfilment. They call out to the virgin Astrea, their opposite and ideal at the full of the moon, in the same breath with which they desire the ecstasy of total submission to the god. The song is not so much a conclusive statement as it is a balanced alternation of images. The first and third stanzas recall the death of the god, the second and fourth counter that vision of supernatural circumstances by evoking the longing mortals feel for union with the supernatural in terms of natural sexual desire. The final song, 'In pity for man's darkening thought' (p. 931), offers conclusions and comments on the action of the play and parallels the structure and content of the opening lyric. The first stanza comments on the implications of Christ's resurrection as the earlier did on Dionysus' rebirth, while the second provides further elaboration on the general cyclical nature of human experience by insisting that human passion exhausts itself and devours its object through its own intensity of feeling. In fact, the final octave suggests a rationalisation of the universal pattern. In both stanzas new images are introduced but the pattern and meaning remain the same. Christ's resurrection is referred to ambiguously as a Galilean turbulence; a fabulous, formless darkness brought into being as the antithesis of Babylonian reason and astrological calculation. As the Syrian acknowledges, Christ's resurrection is a confirmation of the irrational. It is an assertion of emotion and pure feeling which is further emphasised by contrasting the smell of blood present at his death with the objective and academic detachment of Plato's thought or the mathematical perfection of Greek architecture. In the second stanza sexual, artistic, royal, and martial imagery are invoked as analogues of the idea that the flame of man's passion consumes itself in time. Lover, artist, herald, and soldier exhaust their glory and might in achieving their individual ends and so exemplify the eternal cycles of universal experience. Not just mutability but a dialectical flux something like the philosophical principle of Heraclitus determines our existence and experience. The last words of the dialogue mention Heraclitus and paraphrase his thought: 'God and man die each other's life, live each other's death.' (p. 931) Existence is a process of becoming different from or opposite to the original condition as we readily see in the content, form, and structural prominence of the songs.

Related images, both literary and theatrical, reinforce the burden of the songs and help to establish the pattern of recurring ideas which give meaning to the play. The Syrian, for example, reintroduces the imagery of historical cycles which first appeared in the opening song when reporting the fact of Christ's resurrection and commenting upon its implications: 'another Argo seeks another fleece, another Troy is sacked.' (pp. 923 and 925) Repeated laughter also indicates the presence of the irrational. In the first half of the play the Greek laughs ironically on glimpsing Calvary through the window and, later, the Syrian laughs at the realisation that Christ's resurrection is outside knowledge and order as it was then understood. The laughter is finally associated with the worshippers of Dionysus who are outside, and confused with their drumming and rattles. Laughter becomes a revelation of the supernatural as was the case with the clashing of swords in *The Unicorn from the Stars* but retains all the irony and ambiguity of Seanchan's final words in *The King's Threshold*: 'King! King! Dead faces laugh.' (p. 310). Even the verbal image of the phantom with the beating heart is familiar from *The Only Jealousy of Emer* and it does render the abstract idea of Christ's dual nature vividly concrete, as do the highly structured patterns and objective language of the play.

Because *The Resurrection* is more an interplay of ideas than of characters and actions, it is understandable that Yeats cast it in prose rather than verse. In general, poetry tends to elevate ritualistic action through its rhythmic movement and musical intensity. In this particular play there is little or no real action and the prose of the speeches is meant to help ground the dramatic conflict in actuality. The ordinariness of the speakers is important and yet their speech is highly stylised, archaic, and at times, unnatural. Even when they are not making statements of doctrinal importance they are likely to use very formal syntax and rhetorical figures. Their vocabulary remains relatively simple but their function as ritualised principles of the mind is insisted upon through the language they use.

> *The Hebrew.* We can keep the mob off for some minutes, long enough for the Eleven to escape over the roofs. I shall defend the narrow stair between this and the street until I am killed, then you will take my place. Why is not the Syrian here? (p. 905)

> *The Greek.* You need not be afraid. The crowd has begun to move away. [*The Hebrew goes down into the audience towards the left.*] I deduce from our great philosophers that a god can overwhelm man with disaster, take health and wealth away, but man keeps his privacy. If that is the Syrian he may bring such confirmation that mankind will never forget his words. (p. 919)

The prose rhythms are reasonably musical, becoming more regularly patterned at moments of intense emotion, but rarely so much so as to approximate verse. The songs follow the pattern of earlier dance plays. The first and last of them are identical in stanza form even to the regularity of the tetrameter rhythms and interlocking rhyme (abbab). The central song is more flexible in its mixture of tetrameter and trimeter lines as well as the emphatically repeated word – rather than rhyming syllable – in each stanza (*abbab*) which contrasts with the less precise echoes of approximate rhymes. The musicality of language in this play is not a primary mean of expression, rather it creates a harmonious and mysterious atmosphere in which the imagination of the audience is challenged to recreate the significant action.

All the technical features of theatrical production developed for the earlier dance plays are present in *The Resurrection* but physical action and movement are suppressed in order to place the greatest emphasis on the climactic entry of Christ at the end. Instead of insisting on anti-illusionism as in *Calvary*, for example, where the action is said to be taking place only in the tormented mind of the dead Christ, the characters and setting of *The Resurrection* insist on the illusion of stage realism. Although there is a song for the folding and unfolding of the cloth, the description of the scene implies a stage setting and not just a playing area before a wall or curtain. The text, as we have seen, makes an effort to establish both characters and action by association with an actual historical event. The dances of the Dionysiacs are not shown on stage, however, but described or reported to us so that the scene is wholly realised in the audience's imagination. For that matter, the image of Mount Calvary seen through the window by the Greek is also invisible to the audience, as is the confrontation of Christ and the apostles in the inner room. The only physical movement is the entrance of the distraught Syrian and that of the masked figure of the dead Christ who enters through a blank wall and is discovered to have a beating, human heart. In such a static context and following the careful build-up of cyclical and resurrection images, the movement of Christ across the stage or playing area is as striking and significant a gesture as a dance would have been. The other extraliterary element Yeats uses to heighten the effect is the carefully integrated music which is heard from outside. The drums and rattles of the Dionysiacs accompanying their songs and dances merge with the main dramatic action when the Syrian's prophetic laughter in recognition of a new and irrational cycle is picked up by the crowds outside and becomes indistinguishable from the music they play in anticipation of their god's rebirth. In keeping with its subject matter and the dramatic effect desired *The Resurrection* is austerely limited to the barest essentials of production technique.

THE WORDS UPON THE WINDOW-PANE (1934)

Original Publication: Dublin and London, 1934
First Performance: Dublin, 1934

Instead of presenting the passionate dreaming back of Jonathan Swift who is caught between the opposition of Vanessa (body) and Stella (mind) as an anti-illusionistic dance drama, Yeats chose to place those isolated, climactic moments within the framework of conventional stage realism. The inner tensions and conflicts of Swift's personal dilemma are played out against the cultural and social conditions of contemporary Ireland, forming a sharp contrast and a telling commentary on the prevailing debasement of a once heroic culture. The world of the play is founded on lower middle class preoccupations; coursing and shopkeeping, spiritualism and evangelical uplift. The choice of representative characters is fairly evenly balanced. Cornelius Patterson and Mrs Mallet pursue purely materialistic ends; one is interested in being able to continue his passion for horse racing after death since that is his purpose and pleasure in life, the other in her late husband's advice on business affairs. Abraham Johnson, a pious minister of the gospel, is not far behind them in self-interest. He wants to learn the secrets of Moody and Sankey's success and stresses the expenses incurred in his journey from Belfast to attend the seances. He implies that he is not getting value for money because of the bad influence which has been disrupting the meetings. Mrs Henderson, Dr Trench, Miss Mackenna, and John Corbet, on the other hand, are largely disinterested, but Yeats gently mocks both women by having Miss Mackenna closet herself with Cornelius Patterson in order to get tips for the track while Mrs Henderson casts anxious eyes on the donations offered after the supposedly unsuccessful seance. In both cases the quiet comedy is founded in the discrepancy between genteel pretensions and the actual preoccupations of the women. A kinship of character and preoccupation also exists between John Corbet and Dr Trench as well as an opposition of youth and age. John Corbet is a young and sceptical scholar still searching for the answers to the problem of man's relationship with the supernatural and with the past, while Dr Trench is a benign old man of some learning and culture who has found all he needs for his intellectual welfare in the philosophy of Emmanuel Swedenborg. Both John Corbet and Dr Trench are dialectical opposites to Cornelius Patterson and Abraham Johnson and the contrast between the courteous Dublin mystic and the egocentric Belfast preacher is striking. Yet in another sense they are a cut above the others in breeding and social position as well as in learning and culture. They are the only characters in the play who are familiar with Irish history and for whom the nobility of eighteenth century Dublin is real. They alone can place in context and understand the implications of the seemingly random scenes from the past which are played out through the mediumship of Mrs Henderson.

For Yeats, Jonathan Swift is the last passionate hero of the Renaissance and his age is a major turning point for Ireland in the progress of historical cycles. The central question of the play as phrased by John Corbet, is how Swift, a celibate and ageing scholar, could keep the love of two such women. The visionary glimpses we are given of his predicament are of the remorse and torment he experienced. The insistent projection of these scenes as Swift's imagination continues to recreate them from beyond the grave is a classical example of the dreaming back one so often encounters in Yeats's middle and late plays. The conventions of the spiritualist seance, however, make the intrusion of the supernatural much more acceptable to a modern audience than the spontaneous and abstract apparitions in *The Dreaming of the Bones* or *Calvary*. One naturally expects supernatural visitations at a seance and the rather special kind of intervention which actually takes place needs very little justification. The method is certainly similar to that of *The Resurrection* where a familiar pattern of reality serves as a springboard to a stylisation or revision of the original tale and a restatement of Yeats's perennial themes.

Yeats sees Swift's dilemma as an opposition of body and mind. On the one side he is beleaguered by Vanessa, representing chance and passion, and Stella, representing choice and reason. On the other he refuses steadfastly to consummate his personality or beget children, both because of the personal (physical) taint of ill-health or madness and the general (intellectual) taint of madness and irrationality in man. The arguments are outlined by Swift in the two visions from the past and they are linked by repeated allusions to gambling. The room in which the seance takes place and where the words of Stella's poem are scratched upon the window-pane is said to have belonged to friends of Swift. The small sums of money lost at cards about which Swift is said to have chaffed her in the *Journal to Stella* are then associated with this very room and the scene is charged with emotion and ghostly presences. The first intrusion of a past dialogue is of a quarrel between Vanessa and Swift in which she offers him her physical love while Stella offers him another kind of fulfilment. She compares her body to the white dice of gamblers and challenges Swift to take his chances on begetting a mad son, a rascal, or a knave. She warns him that the dice of the intellect are loaded while her body is the common ivory dice and stressed the loneliness of old men without wives or children. Swift's ghostly monologue addressed to Stella begins with a similar statement of his remorse because of her unhappy plight; without children, lover, or husband. Stella's voice is only heard through lines quoted from her poem and much emphasis is placed on the idea that perfection of mind or soul brings more happiness than physical beauty. Swift had actually paid a good deal of attention to Stella's changing looks in his own verse and Yeats uses this as an inverse measure of her perfection of mind. At one point he even has John Corbet claim her to be a better poet than Swift and compare the quality of the lines upon the window-pane to those of Donne and Crashaw.

The daemonic possession of Mrs Henderson by the ghost of Jonathan Swift is more than just a presentation of his personal dilemma with respect to a confrontation of mind and body. It is also a vehicle for expressing the larger implications of historical cycles and the effect of thought on existence. John Corbet's thesis is that men of intellect in Swift's day achieved greater social or political positions and power than ever before and thus established a high point of culture and national character which still survives as an image or model in the present day. Swift's world and its passionate thought is constantly compared to that of Dr Trench and John Corbet who are his modern counterparts (both as old and young man) in the fictional world of the play. The degradation of modern times is set in even higher relief by allusions to Swift's ideals: Roman order and the intellectual nobility of a Brutus or Cato. His own life had been a struggle to recreate those ideals in Ireland, to teach his age how to prolong its youth by knowing right from wrong and listening to the promptings of the heart. He taught both Vanessa and Stella those heroic virtues. A comparison with their latter day counterparts, Miss Mackenna and Mrs Mallet, enables us to appreciate fully the glories of eighteenth century Dublin. Spiritualism and shopkeeping, coursing and evangelical uplift are constantly opposed to Roman order, heroism, and that last burst of passion and idealism in Europe's renaissance which is represented here by Swift, but also associated with such figures as Bolingbroke, Harley, Ormonde, Grattan and Curran. The tragic element in the play is the assertion of inevitability in the degradation and decline of individuals and historical cycles and the personal tragedy of Jonathan Swift is emblematic of a whole culture's failure to consummate its potential. According to Yeats, Swift lived by his ideals and exercised his mind but neglected or denied his temporal or physical being. Growing old, diseased, disillusioned, and demented, his final comment on the human condition is: 'Perish the day on which I was born.' (Yeats, 1966, p. 956)

The conflict and tension between the age of reason and that of a debased modernity is perhaps most forcefully expressed in terms of spoken language. In addition to the contrast between the neo-classical formality of heroic eighteenth century characters and the colloquial off-handedness of the modern figures, there is also a distinction between the diction of the more elevated register of Dr Trench and John Corbet who represent the survival of culture and the language used by Cornelius Patterson and Abraham Johnson. The contrast is as much one of word choice, syntax, and rhythm as it is of content or subject matter.

> *Mrs. Henderson.* [*in Vanessa's voice*] I questioned her, Jonathan, because I love. Why have you let me spend hours in your company if you did not want me to love you? [*In Swift's voice.*] When I rebuilt Rome in your mind it was as though I walked its streets. [*In Vanessa's voice.*] Was that all, Jonathan? Was I nothing but a painter's canvas? [*In Swift's voice.*] My god, do you think it was easy? I was a man of strong passions and I had sworn never to marry. (p. 949)

In a slightly less formal or balanced style we also have the following.

> *Dr. Trench.* I have shown that writing to several persons, and you are the first who has recognised the lines.

> *John Corbet.* I am writing an essay on Swift and Stella for my doctorate at Cambridge. I hope to prove that in Swift's day men of intellect reached the height of their power – the greatest position they ever attained in society and the State, that everything great in Ireland and in our character, in what remains of our architecture, comes from that day; that we have kept its seal longer than England. (pp. 941–2)

And finally there is the speech of lower middle class characters with its pomposities and pretentiousness.

> *Cornelius Patterson.* I never did like the Heaven they talk about in churches: but when somebody told me that Mrs. Mallet's

husband ate and drank and went about with his favourite
dog, I said to myself, 'That is the place for Corney
Patterson'. I came here to find out if it was true, and I
declare to God I have not heard one word about it.

Abraham Johnson. I ask you, Dr. Trench, as President of the
Dublin Spiritualists' Association to permit me to read the
ritual of exorcism appointed for such occasions. After the
last séance I copied it out of an old book in the library of
Belfast University. I have it here. (pp. 943–4)

More significant still is the bathos of Lulu's baby talk. The irony
of an inarticulate child as mediator between the temporal and
spiritual worlds is very effective. Innocence and authenticity is
established along with the capricious irrationality of the
manifestations. We accept Lulu as an unbiased control at the
same time that we find amusement in the incongruity of her
presence. The range of spoken language and contrast of
intellectual levels is greatly extended by her inclusion and by
association we also accept Mrs Henderson's complete detachment
from the vision of the past in which she has unconsciously
participated. The voices of Vanessa and Swift which come from
Mrs Henderson's mouth are indeed uncanny and inexplicable,
especially after the manifestation of Lulu. John Corbet's rational
assumption that Mrs Henderson is an accomplished actress and
scholar reassures the mind for there is no other logical explanation
of the phenomenon presented. The medium, however, denies any
knowledge of Jonathan Swift and proves her innocence by
questioning the young man's assertion that Swift was the chief
representative of intellect in his time, an arrogant intellect free of
superstition. She had seen Swift in her vision as a dirty and
diseased old man which indicates yet another abrupt time shift in
the remorseful thoughts of his ghost. It also gives us one more
example of the fact that thought and existence are one and the
same. The incontrovertible proof of thought projections from the
supernatural to the temporal world is given in the final revelation
of Jonathan Swift, voicing his passionate disillusionment through
Mrs Henderson when she is entirely alone, performing a mindless
household task. This last example of spirit possession is unknown
to any of the other characters and therefore cannot be explained
away. The audience apprehends the supernatural even more

directly than is the case with the phantom's beating heart, which, after all, is only reported by one of the characters.

Unlike the other plays of Yeats's middle and later period *The Words upon the Window-Pane* makes very little use of experimental production methods. Although the central action is conceived and constructed as those of the anti-illusionist dance plays, the intervention of the supernatural world is framed in an elaborately realistic convention. An actual room in Dublin is meant to be reproduced on stage and peopled by figures familiar to the members of the audience who watch from a conventionally darkened auditorium. In the dance plays the mythological or supernatural action is brought into more direct contact with the audience by being played in a normal drawing room or studio without special lighting or scenery and it is framed or introduced directly by the lyrics of a chorus. The eruption of the supernatural into the illusion of reality on stage is as startling and dramatic as the introduction of symbolic characters and actions into the everyday reality of the audience. The presence of Lulu, Swift, Vanessa, and Stella is made very real although they do not actually appear. There is no need for chanting, musical accompaniment, ritual movement, or dance to heighten the effect, because the words and situations carry the full weight of meaning, but song is used as an adjunct to the diversity and contrast of speech levels. At both the beginning and end of the first supernatural intervention, a hymn is sung, at first to create a conducive atmosphere for the proceedings and then to bring a good influence after the interruption of Swift and Vanessa. The seance is at the very heart of the play and the singing does isolate it within the immediate context as well as emphasising its importance. The song, 'Sun of my soul, Thou Saviour dear' (pp. 946 and 951), which is taken from *The Irish Church Hymnal*, is meant to exemplify the general spinelessness and sentimentality of the modern age. It sets up an ironic counterpoint with the vigorous and reasoned heroic couplets of Stella's poem which are quoted near the beginning of the play and repeated at greater length during the climactic scene of the second supernatural manifestation towards the end. Together, the verses and songs serve as a structural feature in the play, subdividing the action into five symmetrical units. In addition, the poem is central to the play's theme and meaning. The action exemplifies the words scratched upon the window-pane which were inspired by an actual eighteenth century couplet on a window in St John Gogarty's Dublin house, Fairfield. Whereas the Victorian hymn gives us a measure of the present decadence, Stella's poem exemplifies a high point of subjective thought, heroic stature, and human passion in cycles of personal and historical development.

A FULL MOON IN MARCH (1934)

Original Publication: Chicago and London, 1935
First Performance: ⸺

Because of the extreme simplicity of its character relationships and the near abstraction of its elements *A Full Moon in March* is open to a number of different interpretations and judgments. In it we have a virgin goddess or queen, an ideal figure of the supernatural world, who represents the spiritual condition of the soul on one level of interpretation and the artist's muse on another. Although she is both cruel and perfectly beautiful, she is incomplete and needs human love in order to fulfil herself and complete her own nature. Her antagonist is a swineherd, a filthy, arrogant strolling singer, who represents the human condition or body, and also the poet or artist. He is in equal need of a virgin spiritual ideal in order to complete his being and achieve an ultimate wholeness. The moment of their encounter is at the full of the moon in March, the time of the vernal equinox, which engenders the child of the winter solstice, image of cyclical renewal. The full moon is always associated with the perfect subjectivity of phase fifteen on the great wheel of Yeats's esoteric system where unity of being is achieved, and March with the moment when one complete cycle of personality or history gives way to another. As the prior force dies, its opposite is born.

The dramatic tension which exists between queen and swineherd is worked out in terms of domination and self-sacrifice. Their relationship is one of natural conflict or opposition and its resolution. Their violent sexual antagonism is made acceptable, however, because it is removed from actual reality to a world of folklore and myth outside time and beyond the rational world. The dramatic conflict is immediately recognised as archetypal and carries the authority and psychological inevitability of the

traditional tale of the disdainful and proud princess who is made
to humble herself by marrying any man who successfully passes a
difficult test. According to Yeats's system, however, intercourse
or intersection between the opposite principles is necessary in
order to achieve unity of being and reunify that dynamic aspect of
godhead which has been projected into the created universe with
the sterile condition of the spirit which remains. Self-sacrifice is
the key to that reconciliation of opposites. The swineherd gives
all, offering himself up to a creative death. He is enthroned and
immortalised as a star. The queen also sacrifices herself to an
antithetical and creative death. She begins the descent into a
mortal and reproductive world of nature through the child she
conceives. The play is a ritual projection of Yeats's metaphysical
vision which reconciles the antitheses of temporal and spiritual
being, male and female, war and love, as well as providing an
analogue or paradigm of poetic creation. The poet sacrifices his
temporal well-being for the ecstasies of creation while the muse as
deathless-image-out-of-time, sacrifices her autonomy and ideal
perfection to incarnate in the world of time.

The progress of the conflict is relatively straightforward and
follows Yeats's usual pattern of symmetrical subdivisions. The
action is roughly divided in two by the closing of the inner curtain
at the point of symbolic intercourse and change of state between
queen and swineherd, while the rising action of the first half is
also divided into antithetical movements. In the first section of
dialogue the inevitability of the encounter and its outcome is
emphasised, yet the queen's dominance is unquestioned. She
anticipates her deliverer and the swineherd seems to be driven by
unknown and irresistible forces. The prophecy of beggars states
that the queen must be won at the full moon in March. The
moment is come and no other man has appeared. The swineherd
is preoccupied by his foulness, the queen by her virgin cruelty and
the authority to choose her lover. He has lost all memory and
attachment to life but is confident of his nature and of his success.
She waits to be moved, to respond intuitively and from the depths
of her being to his song. Suddenly his memory returns and the
ritual being enacted erupts into a pronounced conflict. The
swineherd rejects the offer of a kingdom and exults in the details
of physical sexuality. The queen appears shocked and insulted,
ordering his death. But the would-be lover trusts to the
inevitability of chance or fate (a number on a roulette wheel) and

then tells the story of the woman who conceived because a drop of blood entered her womb. It is obvious that the queen is fascinated by his very foulness, attracted by a nature and condition so opposite to her own. She shudders at the horror of his words rather than at the beauty of his song, but all the same she is moved to accept him in a violent embrace, a union and outcome contrary to the fairy tale ending we had at first been led to expect. The turning point is the swineherd's rejection of his role because of his recovered memory, a doctrinal point which finds its closest parallel in Cuchulain's denial of Fand in *The Only Jealousy of Emer*. The difference is that the queen is not an hour away from her completion nor the swineherd a day away from his. It is, indeed, the full moon in March. The queen has stretched and yawned three times in anticipation of her fulfilment and he is now but minutes from his, with just enough arrogance and capriciousness to spurn the prize he pursues and bring about a climax in which they can unite and exchange states of being.

The second half of the play is turned over to the attendant who substitutes directly for the voices of queen and swineherd after the choral interlude in which parallel legends and examples from history are alluded to. It ends with a sung commentary in pentameters instead of the usually shortened lyric form. The interlude itself is almost exactly the same length as the climactic part of the rising action; from the return of the swineherd's memory to the closing of the inner curtain which suggests the transforming union between the queen and her lover. The final subdivision which comments on that transformation is about one half the length of the initial exposition, giving a sense of acceleration and rhythmic climax to the movement of the play, especially since the greatest weight of symbolic meaning is couched in the three songs clustered at the end.

The song of the first attendant 'He had famished in a wilderness' (Yeats, 1966, p. 986), which takes place during the break in the action allowing the swineherd to leave the stage unseen and the queen to alter her costume, makes two relevant points. The first two stanzas refer to the legend of Dectira and Aodh, but gives a rather different view of the story from that of 'The Binding of the Hair' published in *The Secret Rose* (1897) and reprinted in *Mythologies* (1959). The speaker in the song is Dectira and she twice denies that she was instrumental in the beheading of her lover who had vowed that not even death could stop him from singing her praises. The point is that Aodh's severed head did sing; a miraculous, irrational occurrence did take place. The last two stanzas begin obliquely by speaking of the transfer of power and state in sexual intercourse between mismatched partners. An innkeeper's daughter of Byzantium did become Empress through marriage to Romanus, and women such as Helen of Troy, of actual political power or influence over kings through their beauty and desirability, have experienced heroic ecstasies and abandon through intercourse with a chosen mate, whether king or clown. The song, however, goes on to make the point that that kind of finite experience is nothing beside the miraculous testimonial of a severed head which sings. The queen's song, 'Child and darling, hear my song' (p. 987), echoes Dectira's words; she too denies responsibility for her lover's death and insists that the violent cruelty of his beheading is an inevitable exertion of her prior virgin state. The union they both wish for is creative as well as destructive. She desires the dynamic force of creativity in him and makes love to him, but her sterile spirituality absorbs and annihilates that force in him. In his turn the swineherd sings a song of male–female relationships, but universalises its application: 'I sing a song of Jack and Jill.' (p. 988) The fairy tale quality of the ritual being enacted is now reinforced by association with the world of nursery rhymes. Instead of going up the hill for water and falling back down, however, Jill is said to have murdered Jack, making a successful circuit of the hill; up, around, and back down intact, under the brightly shining full moon of March. Jill not only 'murders' Jack but transforms his beating heart into a star, a thing both external and eternal. Whether taken as an allegory of the soul or one of poetic creation, the relationship between swineherd and queen, first established through ritual action, is now re-emphasised through the complex imagery of the two songs. The play ends in a kind of spoken chorus or commentary which attempts to justify the relationship of motivating force to outcome. Instead of personal statements by the main characters, however, the final song, 'Why must those holy haughty feet descend' (p. 989), is given by the attendants in their own voices. The singer continues the process of generalisation or universalisation which was begun in the severed head's song of Jack and Jill by substituting the images of kings, sages, and saints, externalised and eternalised in Byzantine mosaics, for the queen herself. Explicit questions are then raised. Why should pure spirit which is outside the mire and complexity of the human condition seek to leave its perfected state and incarnate itself in the physical world? What creative force or power mixes the cosmetic rouge or raddle (blood?) with the white (pure spirit?) in the pictures? The questions, of course, are rhetorical since the ritual action has already answered them, and the ironic, paradoxical refrain repeats that answer. The second stanza contrasts the mortal, objective speaker whose heart is savage and sunlit, with the figures in the mosaics who are emblems of the subjective moon. They look out into a purely spiritual universe and inspire an awesome fear in those of us who look on them.

> What can she lack whose emblem is the moon?
> But desecration and the lover's night. (p. 989)

The last stanza continues with the image of the mosaic, implying that the whole play is a mosaic come to life. The attendant asks that the emblem of the moon speak again and reveal the treasures of eternity which are symbolised by the image of pitchers, an oblique reference to the waters of regeneration which Jack and Jill are perennially in search of. In every instance, the songs reiterate and confirm the ritual enactment and they also provide other perspectives and points of view for understanding that action in a wider context.

As in the other dance plays the chorus serves to frame the action and to mediate between the world of the audience and that of the symbolic action. In the same way that the final speeches of the attendants return us to the point of view of the spectators looking at and interpreting the action of the play, their introductory dialogue and song establishes the subject matter and theme. The approach is more overtly anti-illusionistic than usual and they self-consciously create their own roles in a Pirandellian way. They begin by asking what they are to do and how they are to do it. The idea is that neither the subject of the play nor their role in it has been prescribed, but that whatever they do is preordained. They may participate whenever they like in any manner at all, they may even choose the subject of the action. Whatever their choice, they say, that action will follow a preordained pattern because of the all-pervasive scheme of universal order. The induction itself is very brief and ends in a song, 'Every loutish lad in love.' (p. 979) Its antithetical images centre on a stated relationship between loutish lads and the philosopher Pythagoras but includes a refrain which merely juxtaposes the dung of swine and a crown of gold. The unstated link between the pairs of images is perfected love as discovered in the interpenetration of opposites which makes the fool wise and a wise man foolish, which reduces the golden crown to swine's dung and elevates dung to the status of a crown. Such a transfer of states and qualities is exactly what the play is about.

The representative characters who act out the ritual are as much differentiated by language usage as they are by the subject and imagery of the songs associated with them. The queen speaks an elevated, archaic language, formally cadenced and characterised by frequent inversions. The swineherd also uses fairy-tale phrasing from time to time but more often speaks a lean and colloquial modern idiom which is characterised by a clipped rhythm and intentionally awkward syntax. For Yeats it is another turning-point in his development of dramatic language which looks forward to the more radical style of *The Herne's Egg* and *Purgatory*.

> *The Swineherd.* But what if some blind aged cripple sing
>   Better than wholesome men?
> *The Queen.*   Some I reject.
>   Some I have punished for their impudence.
>   None I abhor can sing.
> *The Swineherd.*   So that's the catch.
>   Queen, look at me, look long at these foul rags,
>   At hair more foul and ragged than my rags;
>   Look on my scratched foul flesh. (p. 981)

The interplay and opposition of register, rhythm, and sound patterning give a great deal of variety and liveliness to the speeches of this play and show Yeats to be as creative with modern idiom as he had been earlier with peasant dialect. Although still working with blank verse, he adapts it into a suitable vehicle for contemporary speech and counterpoints its movement with the more lyrical songs in rhymed tetrameters. These, in turn, figure in the play's structure as a sort of poetic subplot, carrying with them their own patterns of imagery and weight of meaning.

The central image of the ritual, as it should be, is visual: the swineherd's severed head and the dances of the queen to the accompaniment of the attendants' songs and commentary. The severed head which sings is obviously another version of the equally paradoxical phantom with a beating heart in *The Only Jealousy of Emer* and *The Resurrection*, while there are also a number of references to the heart as opposed to the head in *A Full Moon in March*. The juxtaposition of the severed head and the dance of destructive womanhood undoubtedly owes something to the fabled dance performed by the daughter of Herodias which had come to figure in the beheading of John the Baptist, although neither is specifically mentioned in the play. The figure of Salome, whether in the painting of Gustave Moreau, the play of that name by Oscar Wilde, or Stéphane Mallarmé's *Hérodiade*, was a very familiar image throughout the symbolist period and Yeats associated it with regeneration myths in *A Full Moon in March* by adding the inevitability of the queen's impregnation and the miraculous transcendence of death which enables the slain lover to sing. The mime is as important as the literary text and the enthronement of the severed head to the accompaniment of drum taps constitutes a symbolic action in itself which contrasts sharply with the actual words of her song. During the song of the severed head the queen mimes her invitation and refusal of the swineherd, summarising the earlier action of the play while the lover comments on its outcome. In the end she dances before the head, now dethroned and placed on the ground to indicate its human qualities or characteristics, at first in adoration but then suggesting their intercourse and symbolically, her change of state as the earlier enthronement had represented his. More and more Yeats had come to use the dance not merely as an extraliterary device to express a complex emotion for which words alone would not suffice, but rather as a means of actually furthering the narration directly or of summarising and therefore establishing it as a theatrical image.

Musical accompaniment, dance and song certainly combine more forcefully and expressively in this play than in any other and sound symbolism is also included at the climactic moment. Both swineherd and queen laugh after the other's song, suggesting both the irrationality of the incongruous events and their spontaneous joy in achieving so perfect a union and harmony. Considering the extreme condensation of the mythic episode and its elaborate structure of symbolic conflict, image patterns, verse, song, music, and dance, not to mention the masks and costuming, *A Full Moon in March* is the most highly developed of the dance plays derived from the Japanese nōh. The only element missing from the form Yeats had created is the use of area staging in a normal living room or studio, but the specific need for an inner curtain suggests a proscenium stage.

THE KING OF THE GREAT CLOCK TOWER (1935)

Original Publication: London and Dublin, 1934
First Performance: Dublin, 1934

Basically, there is not a great deal of difference between *The King of the Great Clock Tower* and *A Full Moon in March*. *Clock Tower* was written first and appeared in a prose version in 1934 which underwent very little revision when it was reworked in verse the next year. *A Full Moon in March* is really a fundamental revision of the earlier play which was undertaken to overcome defects imposed on the original by the circumstances under which it was written. Ninette de Valois had helped Yeats to found a small school of ballet at the Abbey theatre in 1927, providing a teacher and coming herself for a fortnight or so each season with a few students from her London school to help in staging simple dance programmes and the more elaborate plays for dancers. *The King of the Great Clock Tower* was written with her in mind as the queen. Dame Ninette was a dancer, not an actress, and she would not agree to speak from the stage. The queen in *Clock Tower* has no speeches and the direct conflict or antagonism between her and the stroller is somewhat displaced and distorted by the substitution of the king's less immediate quarrel. Although the dances remain almost exactly the same in the two plays, the nature of the exposition is rather different.

The doctrinal emphasis in *The King of the Great Clock Tower*, as we can see from its title, is on time and temporal existence. The queen is a mysterious figure who had appeared at the king's palace exactly one year before and whose origins are still completely unknown. The circumstances tend to recall the Dectora myth which had influenced *The Shadowy Waters* but here the point of view is radically altered. The later heroine is explicitly associated with the annual cycle of the natural world and compared to a sculptured image which mediates between temporal and supernatural reality. In fact, her brooding silence and the king's emphatic reference to it is very reminiscent of the old man's encounter with the woman of the sidhe in *At the Hawk's Well*. At this point the audacious stroller, who also identifies himself as a fool and a poet, bursts upon the scene, wishing to look upon the queen who has become to him such an obsessive image of ideal womanhood that he has cast aside his own wife. The action takes a marked turn at the mid-point of the play after the stroller has accomplished his purpose and seen the queen. He reveals the drunken prophecy that the queen will dance before him and he, in response, will sing to her. He next reveals a supernatural vision prophesying that on the stroke of midnight when the old year dies the queen will kiss his mouth. Incensed, the king orders the stroller's head cut off and the ritual moves on to its inevitable end.

Interpretations of the actions abound, but however different their emphasis, they are not mutually exclusive. The three main characters are certainly symbols or representations of universal principles who ultimately complete their being in a world of time. The king of the clock tower is the dominant figure in whose realm and before whose person the rite is carried out. On one level the queen is the incarnated year, the supernatural force or essence which animates the created universe, and on another, she is the eternal female principle, obsessed by her virgin cruelty and in conflict with man's eternal need to dominate. Her dance with the severed head, its song, and her kiss recreate the renewal and regeneration of nature's cycle as well as the fundamental relationship between supernatural and temporal existence. The king's submission before this image indicates his realisation that the queen and stroller are in no way deceiving him but rather acting out their predestined roles. On another level the queen is a kind of mother goddess, the stroller a slain god of nature, and together they re-enact the central rite of a mystery religion providing us with a new representation of the resolved antinomies in human existence. The stroller is both a subjective antihero and poet, who must die in order to achieve an ultimate union with ideal womanhood and spirituality. He gives up selfhood in order to create. Although not explicitly stated, the stroller is a kind of Dionysus or Christ figure who is linked to the new dispensation of an antithetical gyre or historical cycle through Yeats's radical reinterpretation of Salome's dance. In *The King of the Great Clock Tower* the stroller dies and overcomes death. The queen's role is passive, or at best instrumental, while the king adds little to the ritual except as a vehicle for establishing an element of conflict and underlining the miraculous consummation of universal order. What Yeats gained by giving the queen a speaking part in *A Full Moon in March* and allowing for the possible substitution of a dancer in the second scene, is to rid himself of a superfluous character and give equal attention to the need of the supernatural to incarnate itself in the physical universe.

The queen's song, 'O, what may come' (Yeats, 1966, pp. 999, 1000, and 1001), is one of apprehension and anxiety. Cast in rhetorical questions, it suggests that she understands the stroller's desire but not really the necessity for it. She accepts sexual submission and speculates about the possible effect on her state of being, but nothing in the text actually states or even suggests its precise meaning, her descent into the human condition. The song of the severed head, 'Clip and lip and long for more' (pp. 1001 and 1002–3), on the other hand, is explicit and clear in its celebration of hard-won supernatural knowledge and experience. The imagery and argument are very straightforward. The ecstasies of sexual intercourse are held to be the palest reflection of spiritual pleasures. Crossed fingers in the supernatural world are said to be an unimaginable advance on the physical pleasures of the human marriage bed, and the logical point is how much greater still is the moment of consummation between the dead and the living. Even Virgil, who was credited with the prophecy of Christ's coming in the Fourth Eclogue, had not conceived of such a marvel, and the severed head, which now knows death, is unable to express that miracle directly; 'there's a stone upon my tongue.' The closing song, 'O, but I saw a solemn sight' (pp. 1003–4), which is divided between the first and second attendant, continues to emphasise the actuality of the human condition by careful stages. The principal image is of Castle Dargan, an Irish ruin which is illuminated and peopled in a ghostly vision of past grandeur through the dreaming back of the passionate dead. The reflections which follow consider the mutability and mortality of sub-lunary things. Death and spiritual experience are assumed to constitute the only reality.

The alternative song for the severed head, 'Saddle and ride, I heard a man say' (p. 1005), replaces the indirect description of both ecstatic union between the two worlds and classical allusions, with references to the landscape of the playwright's boyhood home and figures from Irish legend made known to us in his earlier work. The scene is set near Sligo between two mountains and the ghostly figures are called forth to race one another upon the mountain side rather than at the edge of the sea. They are grouped by the common theme of their histories; each experienced passionate conflict and love in this life, merging finally with an opposite and resolving all antinomies in that union. The refrain lines focus on time's relationship to the affairs of men and the approaching inevitability of death; '*A slow low note and an iron bell*' (p. 1005) which places human experience in a wider context of patterned forces and universal order. The alternative song is certainly more closely allied to the image of Castle Dargan which would immediately follow it and also to the vision of Aengus, god of love, which acts as a structural turning point in the play. The opening song of the chorus, 'They dance all day that dance in Tir-nan-oge' (p. 991), links up very well with both versions because it mingles images and exposition of Yeats's esoteric doctrine with those of Celtic mythology. The dancing in Tir-nan-oge, a paradisiacal land of eternal youth, is a dance of pure spirituality outside time. The dancers, who achieve perfect union with one another, are compared to bobbins (perns or gyres), winding and unwinding their experience about themselves like thread. There is no memory of any prior state of separation, nor even thought, in the pure joy of the symbolic dance, however. The third stanza introduces the traditional Celtic images of hound and hornless deer which Yeats took to represent the sexual desire of man and woman for each other and its fulfilment. The idea is repeated and elaborated upon in the image of a woman who will not give up the apple she clasps to the famished man who clamours after it. Woman's virgin cruelty is now associated with the Christian concept of original sin through associations with Adam and Eve and the song confirms the necessity and inevitability of such a pattern within a world of physical existence and time. The man and woman must run ceaselessly after one another over the sea of life within the hearing of the bell which reminds them of their mortality. Reference to a bell announcing major turning points in the dialectical progression of human experience such as the death of individuals, the year and historical cycles are threaded throughout the play and are especially prominent in the songs which both suggest the central theme and comment on the action of the play as well as constitute an important structural feature in the ritual.

The handling of the verse form is only slightly different from that of *A Full Moon in March*. The opening chorus rather than the final song is written in the same pentameters as the main dialogue but distinguished from them by the stylisation of rhyme as are the more contrastive and intensely musical songs of the last section. The interplay of perfect and approximate rhymes in both couplet and interlocking lines is very carefully related to the sense units so that a good deal of extra emphasis and stress is generated. The Blakean verses of the queen's song are written in strict trimeters for maximum impact while those of the stroller and the closing chorus are cast in a free-verse ballad form based on tetrameters, yet with the same intentional awkwardness of syntax and startlingly uneven rhythms used in *A Full Moon in March*.

> *First Attendant. [singing as Head].*
>   Clip and lip and long for more,
>   Mortal men our abstracts are; . . .
>   *What of the hands on the Great Clock face?*
>   All those living wretches crave
>   Prerogatives of the dead that have
>   Sprung heroic from the grave.
>   *A moment more and it tolls midnight.* (pp. 1001 and 1003)

To achieve such effects, a certain amount of inversion and other distortions of natural word order are necessary but the songs and dialogue still retain the freshness and strength of very modern and colloquial language for all the elevated stylisation that is also present. Even in the stroller's set speech describing his vision of the Celtic god of love the interjection of unexpected vocabulary items and frankly colloquial parenthesis challenges the more formal and conventionally poetic aspects of the verse.

> *The Stroller.* I ran to the Boyne Water
>   And where a sea-mew and the salt sea wind
>   Yelled Godhead, on a round green hillock lay;
>   Nine days I fasted there – but that's a secret
>   Between us three – then Aengus and the Gods

Appeared, and when I said what I had sworn
Shouted approval. (p. 997)

It is striking that nature should *yell* godhead or that the gods should *shout* approval, and similarly that the poet's drunken oath in a tavern with its associated images of geese and ganders should also be the mystical prophecy of a holy man as is later confirmed by the vision of the gods and also acted out before the audience. Stylistic oppositions or contrasts rather than those of verse forms and musical composition are largely responsible for the strength and diversity of the play's text. As we have seen, the opening and closing lyrics of the attendants are little differentiated from the verse of the main dialogue and only the songs of the queen and severed head are given alternative and distinctive verse forms. Everything confirms that the point of concentration, after all, is the symbolic dance with the severed head and that that dance expresses ideas which are not contained in the text itself.

In *Clock Tower* the queen's reception of her rude lover is not even hinted at within the text and it is the king (time) who enthrones the severed head, demanding that his consort mock it in a dance. Perched on her shoulder, the head sings and, as the clock strikes midnight, she kisses its lips, consummating their union while the king prostrates himself before the living image of irrational universal forces. The point is made visually and with as little verbal elaboration as possible. In quick succession there is the queen's song of apprehension or fear of defilement, her dance of derision, the miraculous song of the severed head extolling ecstatic union in the supernatural world, and a mimed version of that union. The drama here is certainly more condensed and concentrated than in *A Full Moon in March* but it lacks the theatricality of the second scene in that play which reveals the queen in altered costume and carrying the severed head.

In the prose version (also 1934), Yeats specifies a representative colour scheme for the costumes; red, orange, and black, which further confirms the solar nature of the myth. He also specifies the attendants as chanting in bass and tenor voices. Stage directions for the poetic version, however, do not specify either the sex or musical range of the second attendant who sings the queen's song, but in *A Full Moon in March* there is the stipulation that she be an elderly woman. The effect of such prescriptions on the kind of character created is enormous, and especially so in drama which insists on the archetypal or representative nature of characters as well as their very real and individual existence on stage. Even the masks prescribed for *Clock Tower* strengthen the concept of dialectic opposition on which the ritual is based. The queen is given a beautiful impassive mask while the stroller has a wild, half-savage one covering only the upper part of his face and balanced by a symbolic red beard below. The specification of the queen's mask is omitted from the directions to *A Full Moon in March*, but the opposition of queen and swineherd would also suggest such an obvious contrast. Even the symmetrically placed cubes as thrones and the semi-circular backdrop help to insist on the representative or ritual nature of the action. The emphatic use of drum and gong to underline important actions also contributes to the insistence on symbolism through anti-illusionistic distancing techniques. The drum beats, for example, simulate the stroller's insistent knock on the doors of time, and the gong sounds the tolling of midnight. *The King of the Great Clock Tower* is very obviously conceived in the general pattern of the earlier dance plays and is suitable for production outside a conventional theatre, thus confronting the reality of everyday life directly. In every way it was designed to challenge the audience into a recognition of the truth which lies behind the ritualised stage reality.

THE HERNE'S EGG (1938)

Original Publication: London and New York, 1938
First Performance: ——

Instead of concentrating on a single opposition of universal forces and the image of their reconciliation, Yeats attempted a new departure in *The Herne's Egg*. His immediate source was Samuel Ferguson's long poem, *Congal* (1872), but some commentators have also seen definite signs of assimilation from *Seraphita* (1835, English translation in *Comedy of Human Life*, 1885–91) by Honoré de Balzac. In any case the characters, incidents and images of Yeats's play are once again reinterpreted according to his personal religio-philosophical vision and organised into an original structure which is more elaborate and complex than that of any of his earlier works. His hero, Congal, is followed through a series of interrelated confrontations which are resolved through his death and union with the supernatural world. The confrontations, however, are not necessarily confined to episodes or scene divisions. Instead, they are loosely interwoven within a basically narrative scheme, occurring and recurring as required by the plot. Logical connections are not always stated and to a certain degree meaning is also derived from poetic juxtaposition of images and actions. In the first scene we are introduced to the confrontation between hero and hero, a vision of life as a battle between men. In scene three there is a confrontation between hero and the supernatural, a vision of life as a battle between the hero and godhead. In scenes two, four and five we have the dominant and connecting thread of the hero's confrontation with sexuality, a vision of life as a battle between hero and eternal woman. The last scene gives us the inevitable outcome of this web of oppositions, the transcendent death of the hero as an image of the hero's confrontation with irrationality, a vision of life as a battle between hero (reason) and fool (intuition). Congal's death is the culmination of his career in the play. It is a subtle image of tragic joy in which he merges with his own opposite at a different level from the earlier ecstasies of intercourse with Attracta.

Of course, all this is very private and esoteric. The various themes and images which have been explored one at a time in earlier works are now being integrated into a single dramatic unity whose variety and multiplicity make it a wild and bewildering departure from Yeats's characteristic minimalism. Within the play even the interrelationship of parts is not always readily apparent and our understanding hinges on a recognition of commonality or congruity of symbolic image and theme. The play is a kind of cubist portrait of Yeats's philosophical system, its various themes and images seen as individual cross-sectional views, planes and surfaces simultaneously presented. A further dimension of the complex structure is seen in the mock heroic treatment of the subject matter. Inversions and ironies occur throughout enriching meaning by the addition of unexpected levels of comic improbability and contrast. The total effect is one of antic and earthy irreverence, the aesthetic antiself or mask of the serious philosophy embodied in the play.

Scene one establishes the conditions and values which govern the symbolic world of the action. The image of heroic battle at the point of absolute balance is mimed in a stylised dance while the dialogue confirms the idea that the heroes are at the point of intersection of cones and gyres where all forces are exactly equal. The image is inverted, however, and rendered paradoxical as we begin to see in it an empty gesture in need of revitalisation. The introduction of the music hall or vaudeville joke about the rich fleas who bought a dog offers its own commentary on their situation. Seen from another point of view the heroic kings are fleas who content themselves with a fat, lazy dog of an existence in which they are protected from any and all disturbance. Being no sort of scratching dog, their world offers them neither despair nor ecstasy, neither destructive violence nor creativity. Congal and Aedh are tired of that particular stage of their development and complain that the eternal battle has robbed them of their riches, presumably the very riches which brought them to that present stage of development, their human passion and violence. If they are so dissatisfied, we can expect no other outcome than to see them break out of the present impasse. Scene two offers that new beginning.

Having completed their fiftieth battle, Congal and Aedh wish to prepare for their next confrontation by dining on herne's eggs, but they discover that the eggs are sacred to the great herne, god of that place. Only women dedicated to the god are permitted to handle or eat herne's eggs, and anyone who presumes to steal them falls under the god's curse, both to be changed into a fool and to die at a fool's hands. It follows that Congal defies the god, plays the fool, and later dies at his own hand, but that is not the only, nor even the dominant narrative thread. A good deal of the play is taken up with the question of sexuality in the relationship between Attracta (eternal woman and subjective ideal), the great herne (godhead) and Congal (hero and king). The exposition is reasonably simple. Attracta announces herself to be the herne's bride and Congal calls this madness, a fantasy of female despair which conjures up an image to feed its own sensuality. He alludes to the myths of Danae and Leda, maintaining that Ovid did not guess at the real nature of the women's desire to be forced or of the actuality of the god's penetration. The explicit suggestion is that only a penis suffices, even for a god, and so Congal offers his own, an old campaigner, towards the immediate satisfaction of Attracta's virginal desire. Again it follows that Congal will defy the god by coupling with its intended bride as well as stealing its eggs, but here the metaphor of sexual intercourse as reconciliation between opposites takes on additional depth and complexity.

Not Congal alone, but seven men rape Attracta and she maintains next day that it was the god who entered her embrace. Irrationally, the thunder later confirms the paradox and Congal meekly prepares to meet his end as a consequence of his direct assault on the supernatural. The symbolism of the seven men is vexing, but the early interpretation of Congal as *irajas* (passion) and the others as the six attendant vices of Hindu tradition (vanity, jealousy, sloth, anger, greed, and lust) is much more convincing than that of Christianity's seven deadly sins. Congal is obviously not merely one of the seven men but rather an all-embracing figure and the others are representative aspects of his unified nature. Outside of Mike, who is accounted wise and counsels or corrects Congal at crucial moments in the play, the six are hardly differentiated except in relation to the rape. Their various characters and speeches, however, are not altogether compatible with some of the Hindu vices and another interpretation is required. Considering the plot outline and the suggested relation of Congal to the great herne, it is more probable that the fragmentation of the hero into seven is properly explained in terms of the septenary nature of man, a concept fundamental to the mystical-occult systems of Yeats's time and elaborated from the Platonic or Pauline view of man's being as made up of body, animal soul and spiritual soul. Madame Blavatsky held that there were seven individual elements or fundamental essences upon which and of which all things are constructed. Together they constitute the one universal reality both in the cosmos and in man. Their seven manifestations in human beings are characterised as divine, spiritual, psychic, emotional, astral, psychological, and physical. (See Blavatsky, 1892, pp. 262–3.) When the thunder asserts that it was not the seven men, but rather the god itself, who coupled with Attracta, the paradox makes sense if the seven men are the fundamental essences which together make up the one universal reality in perfected man (Congal) and in the cosmos (the great herne). Earlier, Attracta maintains that the great herne is the sole reality, but the later events of the play insist that the completed hero is an effective manifestation of that reality. Attracta's seven men are as much the great herne's instrument as Danae's shower of gold or Leda's swan are Jove's.

Such an interpretation of the seven men and their role in the symbolic scheme of the play also holds good on an individual level. Yeats is at some pains to list them in order.

> I name the seven: Congal of Tara,
> Patrick, Malachi, Mike, John, James,
> And that coarse hunk of clay, Mathias.
>
> (Yeats, 1966, p. 1028)

In terms of the play's action it makes sense that Congal is a completely developed personality (divine principle). He has broken through the empty gesture of heroic battle by stealing the energising herne's egg and copulating with Attracta as well as overcoming his antiself, Aedh, to become King of Tara and of Connacht. It is also both comically inevitable that Patrick (spiritual soul) should provide the bottle which reintoxicates them for the rape and that Mike (emotional principle) should guide and council Congal. The other figures fall easily within this symbolic system, especially Mathias (physical being), 'that coarse hunk of clay'.

The longish sequence played out between Attracta and her three followers: Mary, Agnes, and Kate also partakes of the same symbolism. Madame Blavatsky's scheme of the septenary nature of man is divided into a lower quatenary or perishable group of essences or principles and an upper triad of imperishables. Attracta is most probably the emotional or passionate essence, the centre of human desire and seat of the mortal as opposed to the immortal principle. The three girls who bring symbolic offerings make up the totality of her lower quaternary nature. All three are promised husbands as soon as Attracta is married and each carries a ritual object. As vital or psychological principle, Mary offers a jug of cream and it is said that she will marry on the same night Attracta does. As an astral or phantom double, Agnes offers a bowl of butter and a honey-coloured lad is foretold as her husband. As physical principle Kate offers a basket of hen's eggs, while a black-headed husband is foreseen for her. Their talk turns to the sexual and spiritual manipulations of the great herne. Possessed by the god, Attracta picks up one of Kate's eggs which she later substitutes for a herne's egg at Tara and so precipitates the drunken anti-heroic combat of scene four that leads to Congal's conquest of both Aedh and Attracta.

Scene three causes an awkward but necessary break between the exposition of scene two and the catastrophe of scene four. We return to Congal and his men making their way to Tara with the herne's eggs. An important factor is established in preparation for the later scene of anti-heroic combat; no man may enter Tara armed. The theatrical point of the scene, however, is the image of the human campaigners vainly trying to stone a god who has no physical body. The great herne flies within their reach but they cannot hit him, neither does he do them any harm in his present feathery form. Scene four follows with the climactic actions precipitated by the god's psychic possession of Attracta and leads us to its outcome in scene six where Congal's apparent sacrilege is seen for what it actually is. In his completed nature as the one universal reality in man, Congal possesses Attracta, the physical energising principle of mortal existence, and in his person(s) the great herne, the one universal reality in the cosmos, also possesses her. During that multiple intercourse, antinomies on all levels are resolved, individualities subsumed into a transcendent tragic joy. The next scene, however, ends with another reminder of the fate in store for Congal, the predestined effect of the god's curse upon him which ends the play.

In the last scene we have the inevitable death of the hero which is the expected outcome of a preordained cycle as well as a re-affirmation of his original heroic stature. A totally new character and set of symbols are introduced in the figure of Tom Fool who drags large stones onto a stage which already contains a cooking pot, cauldron lid, and kitchen spit. As in the case of Yeats's earlier fools, Tom is an antiheroic mask for Congal, intuition or subjectivity opposed to reason or objectivity. In pursuance of the familiar pattern of parallels, he is also given a counterpart on his own level, Johnny of Meath, who can be taken for Aedh's antiself or mask. Like the fool of *The Hour-Glass* Tom is looking for pennies and like Judas in *Calvary* he has taken it upon himself to fulfil the divine ordination of the herne's curse. The images with which he is associated call attention to themselves by their prominence and beg explanation. The fool arms himself quixotically for combat with cooking pot for helmet, cauldron lid for shield, and kitchen spit for spear. It is a spectacle said to have stilled the earlier screams of the peasant women. Later, Congal carries the pot, lid, and spit back on stage and props the spear amongst the stones in order to fall upon it in an ambiguously heroic death. The images are personal and idiosyncratic. The combination of elements is certainly eclectic and most probably derives from the four treasures of Celtic mythology: the Dagda Mor's cauldron of plenty, the sword and spear of Lugh and the Lia Fail or stone of destiny, which were identified as pleasure, knowledge, courage, and power for the 1904 revision of 'Red Hanrahan' in *Stories of Red Hanrahan*. So armed, the absurd fool is invested with the properties and qualities of the four elements of physical creation, at least that is the usual interpretation according to mystical-occult tradition. On another level the fool is also linked to the seven essences in the one person of Congal since he is Congal's anti-self (see pp. 1027–8) and at the same time to the twenty-eighth phase of the great wheel, the phase of the fool, which completes the cycle of an individual existence. Even without a detailed interpretation, the fool is easily recognised as an agent of ritual inevitability and his relationship to the hero's death holds our attention throughout. The confrontation is one of will and fate, both fool and hero assert that they perform their own will but the suggestion is always present that they are merely executing a divinely ordained fate. The ambiguities, oppositions and inversions of both character and action are so combined that no conclusive deduction is possible. We cannot even be sure at whose hand Congal dies since the fool wounds him and then he throws himself upon the spit. In either case Congal dies at the hands of a fool as he was fated to do, and he has become a fool, for nothing can be so foolish, or so heroic, as to challenge godhead. The paradox maintained throughout the play is that god's fate (chance) and man's will (choice) are the same, that Congal's death is a tragic fall in the classical sense but it is also a ritual revelation or apotheosis in another. Congal completes his being by reconciling himself with everything opposite to his nature. He advances from a point of stasis in his development to the point of merging his being with that of the herne.

Like the queen of *A Full Moon in March* the priestess takes the donkeyherd to herself in order to beget a human form for Congal's reincarnation, and she explains: 'if I do [the great herne's] will./ You are his instrument or himself'. (p. 1039) The final twist of the symbolic action is in the qualification of existing expectations offered by the final speech. We understand that Congal is doomed to being reborn as a donkey – Attracta and Corney are too late with their lovemaking – but Corney observes that the donkey carries its young longer than other beasts. He claims that the gestation period is thirteen months, when in fact it is twelve. The detail is too striking to be overlooked, especially when we remember that the thirteenth cone or cycle of Yeats's system is a state of purely spiritual reality outside temporal limitations. It is a stage of freedom from the inexorable dialectical forces of the universe and is experienced by personalities who have achieved a perfect unity of being at phase fifteen on the great wheel, a moment of complete subjectivity at the full of the moon. Congal, like the Christ of *Calvary*, is at just that point of development and the gestation period for his reincarnation as well as that of the forthcoming age, echoes the form of the great year or complete circuit of the great wheel. The last lines are ironic. There is more to show for all that trouble than just another donkey. The hero's rebirth as a rough half-bred beast will inaugurate another era, a new dispensation antithetical to that of the great herne.

As one might suspect with such complicated action and esoteric symbolism, equally elaborate patterns of imagery and language style are used in *The Herne's Egg* to emphasise schematic relationships and meaning. The most important pairs of opposed images are sun and moon, beast and bird, stone and egg. In scene one for example, Aedh reveals that the battle has lasted from dawn to noon and in the next scene Agnes and Kate argue as to whether Attracta and the herne couple in the heat of the sun or blue-black midnight. Congal is under the herne's curse to die at midnight under a full moon and Attracta sings that her brother emerged from the moon while midnight is her mother. The backdrop for scene six is the round, smiling face of a comic moon and Congal confesses himself to be moon-crazed at the point of his death and apotheosis. Congal, like so many of Yeats's protagonists, is an objective solar hero realising his fullest subjective qualities through union with an ideal woman who is a manifestation of the moon. In the same way the symbolism of beast and bird further substantiates this relationship. The donkey is associated with Congal, first as carrier of the stolen eggs and later as the vehicle for the reincarnation of his soul. The great herne is also linked to Attracta sexually by repeated references and explicit imagery while the central erotic act, the rape of the herne's bride, is enacted between Congal and Attracta. These images are doubly emphasised by their visible natures. The

stuffed donkey offers both a comic spectacle and a suitable
distancing from reality to suggest possible symbolic meaning. The
herne painted on the backdrop of scenes one and two establishes
the brooding presence of the feathered god while in scene three its
terrifying attack on Congal and his men is suggested to the
imagination of the audience by the mime of throwing stones at it,
crouching and ducking to avoid its wrath. Later the herne speaks
through thunder and the effective force of its incorporeal presence
on the action is a measure or indication of its actual power. In any
event the imagery of beast and bird is sufficiently familiar from
the poems and earlier plays to offer no serious impediment to
understanding.

The opposition of stone and egg is less prominent than that of
either sun and moon or beast and bird, but nonetheless indicative
of meaning and it helps to emphasise the relationship of
characters and actions. The very backdrop against which the first
two scenes are played includes a rock upon which the herne stands
and references to rocks abound in the dialogue. Stones are thrown
at the herne in scene three and the image recurs forcibly in the last
scene with the fool clearing a level space of large stones as the site
for Congal's death. The stones in this case become an active agent
through associations with the treasures of Celtic mythology and
especially their use as props for Congal's ritual suicide. At first
the rocky landscape is used to suggest the negative qualities of
barrenness and travail in physical existence, but at the end the
image is also infused with a reassuring sense of inevitable fate or
destiny. On the other hand, the eggs, both herne's and hen's,
suggest fecundity and generation in the supernatural as well as
the temporal world. As we have seen, the theft of the eggs is
linked to the rape of Attracta as well as to the defeat of Aedh and
the egg of generation also acts as egg of contention or discord. The
image is very familiar from folklore and fairy tale alike, and these
associations are played upon in the linking of the sacred herne's
eggs with the ritual offering of cream, butter and hen's eggs.

Yet another pattern of opposed images, and one much
exploited for comic effect, centres on the act of arming or
disarming the warriors. The men of both camps first appear
heroically armed and acting out an epic battle. They then disarm
themselves in order to enter Tara where we later find them in
antiheroic and drunken combat with vulgar candlesticks and
broken table legs. In the last scene the fool arms himself with the

anti-images of a heroic and magical tradition in preparation for single combat with Congal and so deflates the conventionally tragic implications of the hero's death.

The two songs which adorn the text concentrate more on the direct exposition of ideas rather than on presentation through imagery. The first is Corney's formulation of the herne's curse, 'This they nailed upon a post' (p. 1018), which is written in a foreshortened ballad form of uneven line lengths, awkward rhythms, and jarring couplet rhymes. Attracta's song, 'When I take a beast to my joyful heart' (p. 1029), occurs at the end of scene four and takes the place of the rape itself. In keeping with the mythic and ritualistic subject matter, she too uses a ballad form and sings of her coming intercourse with the great herne as well as of its paradoxical nature. By coupling with a supernatural bird she will be made pure and she speculates as to whether or not she will be fundamentally changed or transformed by the experience. In fact, there is no evidence that she is transformed by the act, but Congal does advance one step further within his cycle of development through his part in it. The last verse of the song is again repeated by Attracta on her entrance in the last scene. The question about the transfer of supernatural force is appropriate since she is in the act of merging with the spirit world just as Congal is about to experience that union in death.

The songs are written in the same style as that of the dialogue throughout the play and for once do not offer a marked contrast or heightening of lyric intensity. The verse forms of the dialogue range from trimeters to pentameters and generally tend to utilise the shorter, most irregular combinations for moments of excitement or abandon and the longer, more even cadences for moments of reflection or serious thought. The syntax is equally mixed, colloquial expressions, repetitions, and exclamations are often found side by side with poetic stylisation of language and lyrical rhythms. The imagery is correspondingly striking and explicit.

> *Attracta.* Strong sinew and soft flesh
> Are foliage round the shaft
> Before the arrowsmith
> Has stripped it, and I pray
> That I, all foliage gone,
> May shoot into my joy – (p. 1020)

Congal. I am King Congal of Connacht and of Tara,
That wise, victorious, voluble, unlucky,
Blasphemous, famous, infamous man.
Fool, take this spit when red with blood,
Show it to the people and get all the pennies;
What does it matter what they think?
The Great Herne knows that I have won. (p. 1038)

The effect throughout is that of a terse, charged, and very modern idiom which adds greatly to the strength, naturalness, and excitement of the tragi-comic vision.

Another factor which is bound to enter into any consideration of the play is its heavy reliance on extra-literary devices for expressing meaning. In addition to the two songs which are, in themselves, central to the action, the tune of another is repeated in various telling ways at strategic points in the text. 'The Great Herne's Feather' is played upon a flute in order to summon Attracta at the beginning of the play and is heard again immediately after the speech quoted above as the god summons his bride and possesses her. The men of Tara who come to bear away the arms of Congal's men whistle the tune and the fool of the final scene also whistles it as he arms himself ritually for combat. The simultaneous themes of love and battle as the point of intersection between man and woman, hero and hero, or human beings and god is never lost sight of.

Another remarkable feature is the extended use made of movement in the play, especially in distancing effects and comic inversion. The image of chance or fortune as it enters into the gang rape of Attracta is comically presented as seven drunkards tossing their caps at the sacred egg by way of target. The degree of proximity to the cosmic egg determines the random order of their intercourse with her. But this is one of the few scenes in which properties and actions are realistically presented. The men do have soft skull caps on and they do throw them, whereas the elaborately mimed battles of scenes one and four are choreographed so that swords and shields, candlesticks and table legs never touch or make a sound. Even the counting of the seven men who are about to rape Attracta is carried out in the same stylised way and the digits are indicated by musical instruments, either cymbals, concertina, or drums. The stones which are thrown at the great herne in scene three also exist only in the imagination of the audience as suggested by the mimed motions of Congal's men. In the same way the wounds which Congal receives to his mortal and immortal being are indicated by the movement of the spit towards or across his body, but which never touches him. In this regard, Yeats follows the usage of contemporary expressionist theatre in which the absence of realistic properties or the distortion of realistic movement and gesture is meant to provide a greater stimulation to the imagination of the audience than illusionism could do. The mimed battles become visual metaphors for philosophical ideas and Attracta's puppet-like movements, an indication of the god's possession. The enthronement of the herne's egg by Attracta during her mystical possession is another striking example of visual symbolism while the voice of the god intervening in the temporal world as peals of thunder is as strong a sound metaphor as the music which indicates the noise of battle. In all, the various devices used for projecting meaning in this play are consistently anti-illusionistic and compel our attention towards the meaning behind the patterns of action and character. Strangely enough, the play was not conceived in the form of a dance play, although it shares almost all its characteristic elements except for masks and a framing or encapsulating chorus, yet it would not be very difficult to produce in a private room or studio. The cast is perhaps large, but with a simple slide projector aimed at a wall, one could suggest the required changes of scene. Everything else should be evident from the text, extra-literary symbols, and stage business.

PURGATORY (1939)

Original Publication: Dublin, 1939
First Performance: Dublin, 1938

As well as being a play about an individual hero and the consummation of his character or failure thereof, *Purgatory* also presents us with an image of historical degradation and the failure of a nation or culture to complete its being. In many ways *Purgatory* is closely related to *The Words upon the Window-Pane* but emphasis has shifted from the magnitude of Ireland's fall from the heroic ideal to the bleak view of a contemporary impasse and the need for revitalisation, a break with the past and a new impetus or departure. Instead of Jonathan Swift, a heroic figure from the past, and John Corbet, a young nationalist and an intellectual, the protagonists of *Purgatory* are anti-heroic, a degraded old pedlar and his loutish son. The action is very simple and highly concentrated. The two characters arrive at the old man's birthplace, now the ruined shell of a once great house, and the history of the family's decline is very naturally related to the vulgar boy. The desire of a young gentlewoman for a rough stablehand brought about her death in childbirth as well as the destruction of her house and fortune. Echoes of the queen's encounter with the loutish swineherd in *A Full Moon in March* are fairly strong, but rather than a mythic and timeless setting, *Purgatory* is rooted in a very explicit realism. We learn, for example, that the old man had known the house and tree which stand on stage in their prime some fifty years before and that his son is now sixteen years old, the same age he was when he murdered his debauched father in the flames of the house that the drunkard had set ablaze. The time sequence is important for it associates the destruction of house and tree with the cataclysmic fall of Parnell (1889), which split the nation, and the birth of the boy with the foundation of the Irish Free State and the outbreak of civil war (1922). The point being made is that the social and political tradition of the landed gentry to which the old man's mother belonged derived from the democratising principles of the French revolution but its alliance with the ignorance and passion of the working classes put an end to a once heroic and aristocratic cultural heritage.

Purgatory is as much a play about the end of a historical cycle, the moment of blank despair between the end of one dispensation and the initiation of an antithetical era, as it is a personal story. The obvious decline in fortune of the old man's family is an image of a ruined Ireland, its vigour spent and its thought forced in upon its own past. The passionate turning point for both is pinpointed in the dumb-show dreaming back of the long dead girl who realises her desire for the vulgar groom and its consummation while her son and grandson look on helplessly. The ghostly vision of the young girl and her lover in a lighted window of the ruined house is powerful, but there is an even stronger effect in the overlapping points of view. In addition to being aware of the past compulsively recreating itself and unable to expiate its passionate remorse, the audience also sympathises with the understanding and involvement of the old man and boy. The former is present at his own conception by the degenerate man he later kills and experiences this moment from the past in the presence of a debased son who has just tried to rob him. The boy's cry, 'A dead, living, murdered man!' (Yeats, 1966, p. 1048), recalls the beating heart of a phantom which figures in both *The Only Jealousy of Emer* and *The Resurrection*, while his recognition of the horror implied by the obsessive passion being replayed before him is an indication of audience response. The unexpected murder of the boy with the same knife used against his grandfather is a desperate and futile gesture, doubly horrifying in the breaking of deep-seated taboos and also in the calm assertion that the act has purified the murderer's soul. The ultimate reversal, of course, is the sound of hoofbeats indicating that the scene is to be replayed yet again, and no human action can alter its inevitability. The sins of the past go on generating the greater evils of the present. Nothing can alter the process until the original passion has spent itself, until the misery of the living and the remorse of the dead are appeased.

The qualities that have caused *Purgatory* to be one of Yeats's most admired plays is the condensation and compression of his material, coupled with a lucid and immediately accessible realistic plot. The characters, actions and images are both natural and symbolic, moving and meaningful. The carefully orchestrated sequence of action commands our attention and the tortured human condition it reveals evokes profound sympathy. The old man's plight is very human and plausibly presented. The sensational murder and even the appearance of the supernatural are acceptable on stage while the stylisation of language and the illumination of symbolic house and tree adequately suggest other levels of meaning.

There are also very obvious parallels between the character of relationships and imagery of this play and those of earlier works, especially *At the Hawk's Well* in which an old man and a young man also encounter an irresistible supernatural force that dominates their lives. The old man of *Purgatory* is certainly related to Cuchulain, but as an opposite, an anti-heroic figure advanced in age and nearing the end of his personal cycle of development as is the era he represents. Whereas Cuchulain in the earlier plays is saved from fighting his father and kills his only son, the old man of *Purgatory* murders both his father and son in a vain attempt to alter or influence the inevitability of fate and natural order. He fails in one sense, and his mother continues to relive her passion, but in another his failure is heroic, even tragic in the classical sense of that word. The old man assumes responsibility for his condition and acts in such a way as to complete the predestined pattern of his life. His remorselessness and independence from conventional canons of morality are like those of the young man in *The Dreaming of the Bones*, a necessary and heroic quality which justifies itself as a manifestation of universal and immutable forces.

There is no single source for the plot of *Purgatory* as is also the case with a number of plays from this last phase of Yeats's work for the theatre. Themes and motifs have been traced to early works such as *John Sherman* (1891) [reprinted 1969] and 'Happy and Unhappy Theologians' published in *The Celtic Twilight* (1902) and reprinted in *Mythologies* (1959), but a number of familiar echoes from earlier plays also exist and add greatly to the richness of overtones and texture of the piece. The old man, for example, killed his son for the same reason that Jonathan Swift refuses to consummate his love for Vanessa in *The Words upon the Window-Pane*:

> because had he grown up
> He would have struck a woman's fancy,
> Begot, and passed pollution on. (p. 1049)

A ruined house under a curse and a barren pear tree do figure in *John Sherman* but ruined houses are an important image in *The Dreaming of the Bones* and a dry well under stripped hazel boughs is the central image of *At the Hawk's Well*, not to mention the many ruined houses and riven trees of the poems. In *Purgatory* these images are not mere visual signs or indications of meaning, they operate as independent and symbolic characters. The ruined house takes on a life of its own as a ghostly dumb-show is played out in the lighted window and the vision becomes a concrete demonstration of the irrationality which marks the point of intersection between the supernatural and temporal worlds. The tree is isolated, but flooded by a bright white light on the darkened stage after the murder of the boy while its symbolism is asserted by the old man.

> Study that tree
> It stands there like a purified soul,
> All cold, sweet, glistening light.
> Dear Mother, the window is dark again,
> But you are in the light because
> I finished all that consequence. (p. 1049)

Of course, she is not yet a purified soul standing in a cold, sweet light, she is still attached to memory and remorse, but the dispassionate moment of perfect peace and absorption into spiritual existence remains a possibility. The tree which was fat and greasy with life has passed through its purgation to reach a state of abstract purity and so shall we all, the play suggests, in the fullness of time. The action ends with a recurrence of her passionate dream and the old man's prayer for the repose of her soul which again evokes our sympathy for and identification with real human suffering. The ritual action of the play also makes it bearable by asserting that suffering is a valuable part of the universal pattern.

The ruined house and tree are not the only significant images in the play which echo earlier symbols from their works. The bag of money which the boy attempts to steal from the old man is made prominent as they struggle over it. It drops, spilling its contents on the ground just as the window is lit up and they see the ghost of the old man's father. At that moment the boy speaks of killing his father just as the old man had murdered his, and the natural antagonism between youth and age is brought into question as it was in *On Baile's Strand*. The bag of money suggests control of the material world as the pennies the fool begged for in *The Hour-Glass*, the pieces of silver for which Judas betrayed Christ in *Calvary*, or the bag of pennies the fool hopes to gain by killing Congal in *The Herne's Egg*. Control of the material world in *Purgatory* is juxtaposed with spiritual suffering by placing the struggle over the bag of money together with the vision of the ghostly dreaming back. Should the boy kill his father, it would be a victory for the world of nature and materialism, Caesar's world, but the irrational and horrific intervene. The old man kills the boy with the same jack-knife he uses to cut his meat, the same knife with which he murdered his father. The humble and anti-heroic instrument calls to mind the kitchen spit of *The Herne's Egg* as well as its ideal and heroic counterparts in *Deirdre* and *On Baile's Strand*.

Both jack-knife and money bag suggest the presence of objective or material principles in the same way that the ruined house and riven tree are associated with subjective or spiritual experience.

The one feature in which contrast and opposition do not play a very conspicuous role is the language of the literary text. In general the dialogue is cast in accentual verse based on iambic pentameters and often relies on lines of four stressed syllables for emotional heightening and emphasis. The verse is composed with an eye to the grammatical unit of the sentence rather than that of the poetic line and the verse form is less obtrusive than in some of the other late plays. The broken rhythms, awkward syntax, and harsh sound patterns of modern speech are often replaced by a more refined and smoothly lyrical style which mixes natural and colloquial language with educated and elevated phrasing. The old man's speeches, for example, are sometimes measured and regular with an air of elegant yet natural formality.

> They had loved the trees that he cut down
> To pay what he had lost at cards
> Or spent on horses, drink and women;
> Had loved the house, had loved all
> The intricate passages of the house,
> But he killed the house; to kill a house
> Where great men grew up, married, died,
> I here declare a capital offence. (p. 1044)

The repetitions of syntactical constructions and the word house is very effective, as is the delayed subject and predicate in the last line. The old man is not always so well spoken, however.

> I gave the education that befits
> A bastard that a pedlar got
> Upon a tinker's daughter in a ditch.
> When I had come to sixteen years old
> My father burned down the house when drunk. (p. 1044)

The boy's speeches also vary somewhat, ranging from broad dialect to completely neutral and grammatically correct phrasing. As in the case of the old man's speeches, shifts in style are used either to characterise the protagonists or to make a thematic point.

Another aspect of language usage which contributes to the effectiveness of the play is the way in which the old man's speeches continue on in thought and tone without regard to the contrasting interruptions and interjections of the boy. The object of the device is to suggest a depth of preoccupation, almost of obsession, in the old man. He is shown in an intimate relationship with the past which his degraded son does not share. As tension mounts in the old man's mind, his wits do begin to wander and a line misquoted from Rossetti's 'Eden Bower' pops into his head. After stabbing the boy again and again, he sings lines from a lullaby and seems for the moment quite demented by the force of the passion he experiences. In almost the next breath we have his lucid, rational insight into the symbolism of the tree and the pattern of natural order. His personal anguish and passion return, however, as the ghostly vision replays itself yet again. Instead of using contrasting styles as in earlier plays, *Purgatory* relies on a more subtle interplay of emotional states through which the anti-hero passes and which gives shape to both the ritual being enacted and the emotional response of the audience.

With regard to production method there is very little comment to be made. The setting and visual symbols as well as fragments of poems and song have already been discussed in terms of their relation to meaning. The sound of hoofbeats are suggested in the text but need not necessarily be heard by an audience, and in any case they are as realistic and natural a conception as any other feature of the play. In fact, there is no need for any kind of distancing technique or anti-illusionistic device to call attention to symbolic meaning for in this play surface level and symbolic meaning are one.

THE DEATH OF CUCHULAIN (1939)

Original Publication: Dublin, 1939
First Performance: ———

Unlike the limpid clarity of plot and meaning in *Purgatory*, the action and images of *The Death of Cuchulain* require a certain amount of exposition and interpretation before their interrelationship and unity become evident. The hero, Cuchulain, experiences a number of individual encounters in the

natural course of his progress towards death, but the characters he
meets as well as the action and images involved have a good deal
more to do with the author's private philosophy and earlier plays
of the Cuchulain cycle than they do with the Celtic myths on
which the play is loosely modelled. According to Lady Gregory's
version of the legend as found in 'The Gathering at Muirthemne'
and 'The Death of Cuchulain' Emer tries to stop Cuchulain from
confronting the children of the witch, Calatin, in battle because
he cannot survive their enchantments. Emer sends the beautiful
Niamh to sleep with the hero and so keep him from the fighting
but Badh, one of the three single-eyed daughters of Calatin,
assumes her shape and urges him to attack the enemy. The
Morrigu, another of Calatin's daughters, tries to keep
Cuchulain from the battlefield by damaging his chariot, but he
persists and in the third sortie he is mortally wounded by a lance.
He leaves the thick of battle in search of water, ties himself to a
standing stone, and dies. He is beheaded and mourned by Emer,
while Conall avenges his death by bringing back at least twelve
heads of the principal heroes on the enemy side. Yeats uses a
similar sequence of incidents, but by substituting figures from his
earlier plays and carefully emphasising symbolic associations in
terms of human and historical development according to the
phases of the great wheel, he presents the death of Cuchulain as
that of a solar hero passing through the final phases of his
predestined cycle and arriving back at a stage of objectivity and
passivity represented by phase one, the dark of the moon.

Instead of Niamh, Yeats's Emer sends Eithne Inguba, the
earthly manifestation of the subjective ideal at phase fifteen who
figures opposite Fand in *The Only Jealousy of Emer*. Her message is
reversed by Maeve whom Yeats now associates with the deformed
daughters of Calatin by making her one-eyed. After Cuchulain
has been wounded, Aoife, the earthly manifestation of the
subjective ideal at phase one who is associated with Fand in the
action of *At the Hawk's Well*, appears to the hero. And in the third
episode the blind man of *On Baile's Strand* again functions as an
anti-self or mask to Cuchulain in the same way that the red man
and Bricriu of the sidhe do in *The Green Helmet* and *The Only
Jealousy of Emer* respectively. Before Emer mourns Cuchulain in
the last scene, the Morrigu, goddess of war, who is now seen as a
supernatural manifestation of the subjective ideal in the last
phases of a cycle and is an entirely new character in Yeats's plays,

carefully identifies the six agents of the hero's death, just as she had revealed Maeve's magical intervention earlier on. From the radical revision of the original story and the inclusion of additional detail it is fairly obvious that the individual actions have a deeper and wider-ranging significance.

In the first encounter, for example, the hero is not so much taken in by Maeve's manipulation of Eithne Inguba as he consciously acts upon and expresses his own nature and will. He discounts the idea of irrational, magical intervention, whether Maeve's or the Morrigu's, and accuses Eithne Inguba of willingly betraying him because of his failing virility. Even though she is innocent, she is shaken by his detachment and tolerance of a seeming wrong towards himself and she takes his present lack of passionate response as confirmation that he is about to die. Cuchulain will not accept her word and recalls that it was Emer who brought him back to life after the terrible outcome of *On Baile's Strand*. As an immutable principle or idea, Eithne Inguba remains as she was in *The Only Jealousy of Emer* while the more human Cuchulain indicates the necessity of change in the temporal world. He saves her, however, from the natural human consequences of what he believes to be her wild words by proclaiming his own truth: 'I say she brings a message from my wife.' (Yeats, 1966, p. 1056) Never doubting her treachery or the inevitability of his own death, Cuchulain chooses not to save himself. He goes out to challenge his enemies in battle. His will and fate coincide.

The second encounter brings him face to face with an even earlier phase of his being in the person of Aoife, now grown old and white-haired. Because of his six mortal wounds he has sunk into passivity to the point where he hardly knows where he is or what is happening. With Aoife's help he makes the heroic gesture of strapping himself to the druid stone so that he may die upright. After talking of the events which are recounted in *At the Hawk's Well* and *The Only Jealousy of Emer*, Aoife winds her veil about the pillar stone and fastens him to it more firmly in order that his strength does not rekindle before death overtakes him. The symbolism of belt and veil is not altogether clear but coupled as they are with detailed remniscences of two major turning points in Cuchulain's life, the binding process twice acted out on stage implies an attachment to life through passionate memory and remorse. The belt and veil are obviously masculine and feminine counterparts while the standing stone has both ritual and erotic overtones. The winding and binding itself also calls to mind the familiar images of pernes, bobbins and mummies wound round with the threads or bands of passionate experience on earth which are unwound and relived during the process of dreaming back after death. In any case Cuchulain and Aoife are engaged in just that sort of reliving of the past during the entire scene and they show a distinctly dispassionate attitude towards it because of the distancing of time.

The third encounter is with the blind man of *On Baile's Strand*, the anti-heroic counterpart of Conchubar or reason and material self-interest in that play. It is he who actually kills Cuchulain (rather than Eithne Inguba, Aoife, or Maeve) and the brief dialogue between the two establishes the tragi-comic images of twelve pennies, begging bag, and kitchen knife as well as the good sense of the blind man. The Judas of *Calvary* betrays Christ for a bag of silver, the fool of *The Herne's Egg* kills Congal for a bag of pennies and the old man kills his son over a bag of money in *Purgatory*. Pennies are an ironic inversion of heroic values and the number twelve is significant in Yeats's system as there are twelve cones or cycles in a complete series of physical existences and the thirteenth constitutes a state of purely spiritual reality outside temporal limitations. The bag into which the blind man will put Cuchulain's head is the same one he uses for the scraps he begs at kitchen doors and the knife which cuts off that head is already sharpened because the blind man uses it to cut his food. The bag, and perhaps Aoife's veil as well, was suggested by the silk cloth in which Emer wraps the washed head of Cuchulain in Lady Gregory's version of the tale while the humble knife is closely allied to the kitchen spit of *The Herne's Egg* and the jack-knife of *Purgatory*. Each is an ironic symbol of the universal paradox which results from the intersection of antinomies, and Cuchulain's death is just such a merging of opposites. The point is made symbolically in the final scene which contains only the speech of the Morrigu and Emer's dance.

The dominant images of the final scene are the black parallelogram which represents Cuchulain's severed head and the six smaller ones as opposed to the twelve or more in authentic versions of the legend, which are the heads of his enemies. Each of the six is held responsible for one of the hero's mortal wounds. It is difficult to accept the suggestion that the six heads represent the children of Calatin, three sons and three daughters, since the Morrigu's speech identifies them all as male. A more consistent interpretation is to link the parallelograms with the essences of the septenary nature of man as they had appeared in *The Herne's Egg* where Congal was the complete hero and pure spirit at one with the Absolute as a radiation from it while his six lesser emanations extend down to the base physical body which is the vehicle of all other principles during human existence. Cuchulain, like Congal, dies at his own hand in the sense that the blind man is his anti-self or mask with which he (as fool) is uniting, just as Aoife, on another level, is another of his anti-selves and a possible touchstone in his death. The point of the ritual is to present the preordained actions which fulfil Cuchulain's destiny, complete his being, and permit him to die in the body as a prelude to union with the supernatural when his attachment to human passion has been purged away. The correspondence between the Morrigu's identification of the six men and Madame Blavatsky's definitions are exact; the youthful lover is the physical body, and the vital principle in intercourse with Maeve (here linked with the Morrigu as an earthly manifestation of the subjective ideal in the last phases of an objective hero's life) gives birth to both phantom double and the desire or passion of mortal man. The men of no account are intellectual and spiritual principles which have no bearing on the life of the body and have crept in when the composite physical being was weakening, thus hastening the decline of his human or temporal nature. After all, it is only the degradation of physical death which Cuchulain experiences. The wounds are the progressive stages towards the realisation of higher faculties and rebirth. In her dance Emer rages against Cuchulain's progressive decline as physical man and also celebrates the triumph of his development towards pure spirit. The final image is the apocryphal song of the bird into whose soft, feathery shape Cuchulain's soul has returned. The mime itself is another version of the dance performed with a severed head in both *The King of the Great Clock Tower* and *A Full Moon in March*, not to mention other references to severed heads and miraculous life among the dead in even earlier works.

The scheme of the play's construction is based on the phases of the great wheel and images closely associated with them. For example, bird imagery is central throughout. The soul of Cuchulain, a solar hero, is represented by a bird at his death, and the various manifestations of the subjective ideal he pursues throughout his life are also associated with birds. In the first encounter the choice of Eithne Inguba brings to mind the action of *The Only Jealousy of Emer* with its imagery of sea shell and sea bird and Cuchulain's closest approach to unity of being halfway through his progress round the great wheel. In terms of his approaching death which is the present subject, the scene shows him entering on the first of the final three phases of the cycle, that of the hunchback in which the individual seeks knowledge of isolated lives and actions in relation to their source and supersensual unities rather than in relation to each other. The hero perceives their deformities and inadequacies with great clarity. That phase marks the beginning of self-realisation and is characterised by the desire to understand rationally and to judge objectively. As he enters on the final moments of his life, Cuchulain experiences the breaking of strength and an intensely violent opposition to Eithne Inguba, a figure of the subjective fifteenth phase in which one finds unity of being. In the second encounter we turn to Aoife whose symbol is the hawk, an objective image closely associated with the opening phases of a cycle. Naturally, the action of both *At the Hawk's Well* and *On Baile's Strand* is discussed at some length. In terms of his approaching death Cuchulain is now entering on the phase of the saint in which renunciation and an acknowledgment of the need for expiation dominate. The individual perceives the true source of his total life and his joy is in complete passivity, allowing past experience to flow in upon him and express itself through his acts and thoughts. The dialogue between himself and Aoife, even the winding of the veil about him, present us with a ritualised image of this state. In the last of the three encounters the blind man of *On Baile's Strand* is Cuchulain's antagonist but he is not associated with bird imagery. Maeve, however, and the Morrigu who close the action, have figured in the action from the beginning; Maeve as implacable enemy and the Morrigu as protector. The two figures share the deformity of eye which marks their supernatural powers. Maeve is consciously associated with Fand, woman of the sidhe and hawk-woman of the air while the Morrigu is crow-headed. According to *A Vision* she is the image of a subjective ideal, the antithesis of the solar hero in the last phases of human existence. In terms of progress on the great wheel Cuchulain has now entered on the phase of the fool in which oblivion is sought and the goal is to become his own opposite. The individual in this phase experiences fear and envy of anyone who can act effectively or with intelligence. The blind man (rather than Maeve or the Morrigu) is chosen as the agent of death because he alone reflects Cuchulain's anti-self and recalls the action of an earlier episode in the hero's life. As in the case of the other two encounters, the dialogue, symbolism, and stage business constitute a dramatic image of the description given for that phase in *A Vision*.

In its formal features *The Death of Cuchulain* closely echoes *Calvary* as does its theme, yet it also bears a close resemblance to *At the Hawk's Well*. Here, the hero encounters a supernatural manifestation of the subjective ideal at the site of a magical pool and standing stone instead of a dry well and leafless trees. In the present fictional world the cycle is complete, however, and the fulfilment of personality becomes possible. Both Cuchulain and the supernatural world are now ripe for unification and the recurrence of references to supernatural activities and needs are threaded through the entire work. Another of the features which sets this play apart from all other dance plays is the handling of the chorus. Instead of an integrated chorus of musicians or characters related to the main action, appealing to the imagination of the audience and providing it with relevant images and commentary, *The Death of Cuchulain* has a choric introduction and closing which are antithetical to the main action and even to each other. The old man who speaks the prologue is derived from the original introduction to *The King's Threshold* of 1903 (see pp. 313–14) but he is now a sober and serious character rather than a creature of farce. The speech is cast in prose instead of the usual heightened verse and the intention is anti-illusionistic. The audience is addressed directly and told frankly what to expect; their imagination is not much appealed to, nor their intellect. Yeats's familiar prejudices concerning his romantic subject matter and an aristocratic theatre are presented and gently mocked as the old man warms to his subject and becomes over-excited. The second half of the prologue concentrates on the anti-illusionistic aspects of the production, its use of music, song, dance, and stylised stage properties to produce a hieratic and mythological image which suggests something beyond itself. The introduction directs the attention of the audience to the aesthetic means employed in creating that image and suggests the kind of meaning that should be looked for. The final chorus is even more startling and out of character with Yeats's usual practice. Ragged modern musicians explode on the scene of a ritualised myth, forcing a relationship between the action of the drama and contemporary life. The song, 'The harlot sang to the beggarman' (pp. 1062–3), is exactly what we are led to expect from the old man's prologue. The harlot sings of ideal heroes and warriors from a mythological past, of actual men and their sexual passions in the present, of the ambiguity of loving and loathing which she experiences. The point of the lyric is realised in the second half where the first octet poses rhetorical questions about the individual's relationship to spiritual or ideal reality and the second, about physical or material experience. The point of contact between the two is the image of the Easter Rising of 1916 and heroic resistance in the Dublin Post Office. The song suggests that the spirit of Cuchulain inspired the revolutionaries, and that the mythic hero possessed the physical bodies of the nationalists. His is a perfect or ideal body, but unimpressive to an old man preoccupied with spiritual ideals. The only reconciliation between the two is in an artifact, the statue of Cuchulain by Oliver Sheppard which is an image of the ideal physical body and symbolises a perfect spiritual wholeness in Yeats's mind such as the play tries to present as a dramatic ritual.

Rather than isolating the action and adding lyrical intensity to its rhythmic composition, the choruses of *The Death of Cuchulain* are an integral part of the rhythmical development. The prose prologue is followed by the fairly regular blank verse of the main action and ends with the shortened lines and more intense lyricism of the song's tetrameters. Throughout, there is a progressive heightening of verse form which characterises the developing emotion and carries it to a climax at the end of the play. The language of the dialogue is relatively free of archaisms and obvious poetic locutions. The vocabulary is simple, the syntax natural, if not exactly colloquial, and sense units tend to coincide with line lengths, having the effect of imparting ideas in short emphatic bursts.

> *Cuchulain.* You thought that if you changed I'd kill
>   you for it,
>   When everything sublunary must change,
>   And if I have not changed that goes to prove
>   That I am monstrous.

Eithne. You're not the man I loved,
That violent man forgave no treachery.
If, thinking what you think, you can forgive,
It is because you are about to die. (p. 1055)

The style remains reasonably consistent through the second encounter but in the third, the rhythmic regularity gives way to an accentual verse form based on five stressed syllables to the line with irregularly scattered unstressed syllables as demanded by the sense and the duration of the musical phrase. Tension and human passion are suggested by more abrupt and broken rhythms which communicate the emotion of the piece and lead up to the symbolic dance and bird song which is then confronted by its opposite in the harlot's song at the end.

Blind Man. They say that you are weak with wounds.
I stood between a Fool and the sea at Baile's Strand
When you went mad. What's bound about your hands
So that they cannot move? Some womanish stuff.
I have been fumbling with my stick since dawn
And then heard many voices. I began to beg.
Somebody said that I was in Maeve's tent,
And somebody else, a big man by his voice,
That if I brought Cuchulain's head in a bag
I would be given twelve pennies; I had the bag
To carry what I get at kitchen doors,
Somebody told me how to find the place;
I thought it would have taken till the night,
But this has been my lucky day. (pp. 1059–60)

Whereas the larger composition of language and verse form expresses the emotional outline or movement of the play, the features of its stage production are directly related to its symbolic meaning. The magic pool and pillar stone, Cuchulain's belt and Aoife's veil, the blind man's knife and bag, the weird appearance of the crow-headed Morrigu, the stylised parallelograms representing severed heads, and the few faint bird notes indicating the transmigration of Cuchulain into the supernatural world do not require further elucidation. The ideas or forces they represent are evoked by their visible or audible presence and Yeats avoided the temptation to explain or define them in the text. The prologue contains all the outside help we can expect in unravelling the meaning of the play. The action itself is clear enough and certainly significant in terms of Yeats's perennial themes or earlier aesthetic forms. Although somewhat private and obscure in its detailed relation to the phases of the great wheel, the musical composition, mythic underpinnings, and reliance on dance help right the balance and render the play more accessible than some of its more radical predecessors. The use of instrumental music, in this case provided by the pipe and drum of street musicians at an Irish fair, is particularly effective. It acts as a focus of emphasis when punctuating important speeches and actions within the body of the play and also expresses an antithetical time and temper when accompanying the harlot's song at the end. Emer's dance is equally expressive and offers no impediment to understanding so long as one recognises her as an objective solar heroine and the antithesis of the subjective lunar ideal which Cuchulain pursues throughout his life. He must unite with Aoife, Fand, Eithne Inguba, and Maeve in order to reach spiritual wholeness, just as he must develop each essence or element of his septenary nature. Yet every victory brings him closer to death. The women he encounters in the play are instruments of his death just as the symbolic men whose severed heads Emer rages against are also responsible for it. That death, however, is an ultimate victory, a tragic joy and fulfilment of the universal pattern, an apotheosis and transcendence of human limitations.

5   Conclusion

The enormous diversity of themes and subject matter, forms and styles in Yeats's plays present a very specific problem of approach as well as of interpretation and understanding. A number of critics concentrate on Yeats's esoteric philosophy as an end in itself and write about *A Vision* as though it were a sacred text. Such a view tends to emphasise Yeats's importance as a polemicist rather than a playwright and to ignore the dramatic qualities of his work for the theatre. It is far more sensible to take the system as a schematic arrangement of human experience which provides images and metaphors for poetic drama rather than a mystical hieroglyph or mandala. Readers should aim at working out an interpretation of symbols and structures as they emerge or develop in the plays and present images of either sociological or psychological reality. Another group of critics is preoccupied with the creative role of myth and the ideal of an archetypal culture hero which pervade the plays, while still others concentrate on the development of dramatic form and technique. Yeats's creative experiments with symbolic and archetypal ritual for the theatre have attracted a good deal of interest as has his redefinition of tragedy. It is natural for critics to isolate particular themes, subject matter, or literary techniques for research. Students, on the other hand, should be more committed to a consistent and balanced reading of the plays than to the pursuance of a specialised thesis. Even considering the diversity of themes and subject matter, forms, and styles among Yeats's plays, a consistent reading is certainly possible, as is a general summation of his total achievement. Evidence for such a view is found in the singular direction and force of artistic development which existed throughout his long writing career, regardless of the particular dramatic conception or mode being used at any given stage of that process.

As in the poetry, which is always closely allied to the drama of the same period, the early plays celebrate an idealised spiritual existence which is the unchallenged, although sometimes unconscious, aspiration of the world-weary characters. In the more mature later plays such overt longing for the fulfilment of a supernatural existence is replaced by a celebration of the passion or ecstasy which transcends or justifies the suffering of the human condition. The change is perhaps more a fundamental shift of emphasis than anything else since passion and ecstasy are always prominent in the individual's progress towards spiritual fulfilment. The shift of emphasis is as common to the realistic plays which present sociological or historical reality as to the anti-illusionistic works which tend to project a ritualistic or psychological reality. Whether it is Mary Bruin joining the fairy child in *The Land of Heart's Desire* or Deirdre enshrining herself in myth through heroic acceptance of fate, the point is the individual's translation to an ideal state out of time. On the other hand, the contending features of Jonathan Swift's passionate dilemma in *The Words upon the Window-Pane* as well as those of the old man in *Purgatory* actually characterise important turning points for their respective ages and societies. In the same way Forgael's escape into an ideal existence or state of mind in *The Shadowy Waters* is the point of the passionate union with Dectora, while that between queen and swineherd in *A Full Moon in March* or Congal and Attracta in *The Herne's Egg* is but a moment's transcendence and justification for the degradation and death which inevitably follows. Stated in this way it would seem that the early and late plays are diametrically opposed, but in fact, the actual shift of emphasis is less radical and profound than it would appear. Yeats had always been interested in the relationship between spiritual and physical existence. At first he presented the spiritual ideal as a miraculous intrusion into physical reality, an intervention from above. Later he also began to see it as a manifestation or development from within the consciousness of the individual. The early plays concentrate on creating realistic fictions and archetypal situations which reflect the relations between the natural and supernatural worlds. Yeats's drama of the middle period begins to experiment more forcefully with anti-illusionism and frankly imaginative constructs. It shows much more interest in the heroic stature of representative individuals. As his religio-philosophical system becomes more detailed and explicit, his dramatic situations and schemes of character relationships tend to reflect the outline of forces which he believed determine human personality and history. Whether concentrating on the progress of an individual or of a culture, the metaphor of cones or gyres, which make up the great wheel of existence, enables Yeats to focus on a number of different passionate moments and turning-points in which cosmic fulfilment through a merging of opposites is either achieved or not achieved. In the later plays the related idea of progress on the great wheel as a continuum of development is more prominent than the individual moment of decision. In these works a number of characters pass through more than one stage of development, or different stages are contrasted with one another. The same symbolic relationships, however, recur time and again throughout his career as a dramatist. A young man and an old man in conflict over a woman is perhaps the most common but the natural antagonism of reason (or objective action) and intuition (or subjective creativity) is all-pervasive as well.

In selecting subject matter for the plays, Yeats also shows a marked change of focus which reflects the progressive shift in thematic concerns. For his earliest plays he chose obscure Irish folk tales – generally stories which were virtually unknown to his audiences and for the most part insignificant in terms of impact on a national or cultural consciousness. For Yeats, their appeal lay mainly in some vision of an ideal or supernatural reality. With such plays as *The Shadowy Waters*, *On Baile's Strand*, and *Deirdre*, the authority and basis for Yeats's dramas shifts from the folktale to epic cycles, from traditional peasants to the culture heroes of the ancient Irish people. In the same way that the natural and supernatural worlds are inherently antithetical to one another, so are the worlds of peasant and hero. Up to the first of the dance plays (1917) those worlds were often contrasted as representative poles of reality, sometimes even within a single play. In the middle plays, however, the general emphasis is on heroic action as an ideal or model for human behaviour and the peasant element is replaced by a more realistic common man who begins to emerge as a true antihero. The beggar-tramp or itinerant tinker, actor, and outlaw of early twentieth century society replaces the peasant as the mask or anti-self of the hero. The shift tends to focus attention on social realities with which modern theatre audiences can more easily sympathise. In the late plays subject matter is purposefully diversified to include more archetypal and regenerative cycles of action. Dramatic images and character relationships which are more closely associated with myths as embodied in fairy tales rather than folklore or epic cycles, occur in such works as *The King of the Great Clock Tower, A Full Moon in March,* and *The Herne's Egg.* The actions and speech of these archetypal figures also tend to identify them as contemporary antiheroes.

In the same way that Yeats's themes and subject matter evolved along the same lines, the development of the dramatic techniques he uses to present his visions of the relationship between natural and supernatural reality provides yet another parallel strand. Yeats's early dramatic fables rely on the authority of antique forms of construction, especially classical Greek tragedy and medieval miracle or morality plays. He also experimented briefly with the constructional features and acting styles of contemporary symbolist drama as practised by Maeterlinck and Villiers de l'Isle-Adam but finally evolved a new and personal dramatic form in the plays for dancers which were influenced by classical Japanese nōh drama. Towards the end of his career the characteristic features of the dance plays underwent further development and adaptation under the influence of contemporary expressionist drama and its production methods. Here again the general line of development is quite clear. At the outset the focus of concern is on literary construction, the organisation of realistic subject matter in some way other than the logical and progressive narrative of traditional drama in English. The difficulty was in projecting an adequate representation of the supernatural so that Yeats finally turned to more imaginative and anti-illusionistic methods. By 1910 all sorts of techniques for the direct presentation of imaginative and archetypal action had been tried out: music, song, mimed movement, dance, masks, colour symbolism, and stylised settings, but without much success. The catalyst which led to a successful integration and structuring of such elements within a lyrical or poetic composition was Yeats's introduction to the Japanese nōh in 1913. The plays for dancers constitute a new departure in theme and subject matter as well as in dramatic composition. Yeats's understanding of nōh was far from complete but it offered him both authority for his experiments and a general conception of poetic construction and anti-illusionistic production which he could interpret and redesign to suit his own needs. Above all, what little he understood of nōh justified his own dramatic endeavours and encouraged him to consider realism and comedy as both viable and compatible modes of dramatic expression. Yeats's success, with the dance plays and other radical experiments is actually very similar to that of nōh. Through its example, he too was able to harmonise subject matter and symbolic design by organising dialogue and action into a lyrical composition which expresses a concrete and total image of a single emotion. The form proved just as valid when the subject matter was serious and realistic as when comic and expressionistic. Even in the last plays where a multiplicity of themes and actions is introduced, the same harmony of subject matter and symbol design obtains.

In order to appreciate Yeats's development as a dramatist, it is also important to understand the way in which such a coherent dramatic image is created. In addition to recognising the single moral or philosophical conviction around which the play is built, or the symbolic design of character relationships and action, the part played by language rhythm or musical composition and extraliterary production devices must also be considered. And these factors should be taken into consideration in the case of individual plays as well as in terms of Yeats's changing views and methods throughout his long career. From the very beginning Yeats contrasts the language of a peasant dialect and elevated heroic speech, but he turns more and more to the abrupt directness of a contemporary colloquial idiom as a counterpoint to the natural rhythms and word choice of his later heroes. The early combination of prose and verse gave way to one of shortened lyrics and natural speech rhythms, in either mixed line lengths or emphasised by the increased formality of rhyme. Whereas songs had been used as secondary features for diversity and ornamentation in the early plays, towards the end of his career they became a principal means of exposition and communication of emotion. Similarly, the use of instrumental music, mime, and dance which had always played some part in Yeats's dramas, became increasingly central to meaning throughout his middle and later plays. Whatever narration or multiplication of action had been retained in the early pieces is replaced in the later work by the direct presentation of songs and dances as dramatic images of the emotions or ideas to be communicated. Even the verbal imagery of the earlier plays gives way to physical stage properties or stage pictures which themselves communicate meaning, independent of the dialogue. Strangely enough, the verbal imagery of the later songs is often obscure while the total emotion expressed by the song remains clear and meaningful in its context. Dances and mimed actions are often performed without an accompanying narration. The effect of these developments is to place greater emphasis on the visual and aural possibilities of theatrical presentation. Such features are also carefully harmonised within a rhythmic structure which moves from level to level of intensity until its lyrical outline reaches a climax supported by stage pictures, music, and song, as well as mime and dance. Beginning with rhythmic dialogue and character conflict, stages of logical development are integrated with both archetypal and theatrical images in order to achieve a unified and concrete representation.

For a good many reasons Yeats's plays will never be popular, but it is not too difficult to see what he was trying to do.

> Take anything you will – theatre as speech or a man's body – and develop its emotional expressiveness, and you at once increase its power of suggestion and take away from its power of mimicry or of stating facts. The body begins to take poses or even moves in a dance . . . Speech becomes rhythmical, full of suggestion, and as this change takes place we begin to possess, instead of the real world of mimics, solitudes and wildernesses peopled by divinities and daimons, vast sentiments, the desires of the heart cast forth into forms, mythological being, a frenzied parturition. (Bradford, 1966, p. 293)

References

Balzac, H. de (1885–91) *The Comedy of Human Life*, trans. K. P. Wormeley (Boston: Roberts Bros. and London: Routledge & Sons, 1886–91).

Blavatsky, H. P. (1892) *The Theosophical Glossary* (London: Theosophical Publishing Society).

Bradford, C. B. (1966) *Yeats at Work* (Carbondale: University of Southern Illinois).

Castiglione, B. (1967) *The Book of Courtier*, trans. G. Bull (Harmondsworth: Penguin).

Darwin, C. (1859) *On the Origin of Species* (London: John Murray).

Ellis, E. (1895) *Sancan the Bard* (London: Ward & Downey).

Furguson, S. (1872) *Congal* (Dublin & London: no pub.).

Gregory, I. A. (Lady) (1902) *Cuchulain of Muirthemne: The Story of the Men of the Red Branch of Ulster* (London: John Murray).

——— (1971) *Collected Plays*, 2, ed. Anne Saddlemeyer (London: Oxford University).

Jeffares, A. N. and A. S. Knowland, (1975) *A Commentary on the Collected Plays of W. B. Yeats* (London: Macmillan).

Lespès, L. (1865) *Les Matinées de Timothée Trimm* (Paris: Librairie du 'Petit Journal').

Nietzsche, F. (1909) *The Birth of Tragedy*, trans. W. Haussmann, *The Complete Works of Friedrich Nietzsche*, 1 (Edinburgh & London: J. N. Foulis).

Synge, J. M. (1962) *Collected Works*, ed. Robin Skelton (London: Oxford University).

Unterecker, J. (1959) *A Reader's Guide to William Butler Yeats* (New York: Farrar, Straus & Giroux).

Waite, A. E. (trans.) (1886) *The Mysteries of Magic: A Digest of the Writings of Eliphas Lévi* (London: Redway).

Wheelwright, P. (1959) *Heraclitus* (Princeton: Princeton University).

Wilde, J. F. S. (Lady) (1887) *Ancient Legends, Mystic Charms and Superstitions of Ireland* (London: Ward & Downey).

Wilde, O. (1948) *The Works of Oscar Wilde*, ed. G. F. Maine (London & Glasgow: Collins).

Yeats, W. B. (ed.) (1888) *Fairy and Folktales of the Irish Peasantry* (London: Wm. Scott).

——— (1952) *The Collected Plays of W. B. Yeats* (London: Macmillan).

——— (1955) *Autobiographies* (London: Macmillan).

——— (1959) *Mythologies* (London: Macmillan).

——— (1961) *Essays and Introductions* (London: Macmillan).

—— (1966) *The Variorum Edition of the Plays of W. B. Yeats*, ed. R. K. Alspach (London: Macmillan).

—— (1969) *John Sherman and Dhoya*, ed. R. Finneran (Detroit & London: Wayne State University).

—— (1974) 'Is the Order of R. R. & A. C. to Remain a Magical Order' in G. M. Harper (ed.), *Yeats's Golden Dawn* (London: Macmillan).

Further Reading

There is no great lack of published material on W. B. Yeats or, for that matter, on his involvement with the theatre. The titles included below have been selected as introductions to the relevant areas of study and basic points of departure for further reading; each contains book lists and other suggestions toward a deeper and more thorough understanding of Yeats's plays.

Background Information and Scholarly Tools

Collections of letters and biographies are indispensable sources of information about the relationship between a playwright and his work. A number of such collections and publications have appeared over the years and are readily discovered in any library card catalogue or published bibliography. At the present time both a complete collection of Yeats's letters and a new biography are in preparation which will bring together all of the material now available as well as offering new information and fresh insights. There are also a number of scholarly tools which are vital to any attempt at further study.

Russell K. Alspach (ed.), *The Variorum Edition of the Plays of W. B. Yeats* (London: Macmillan, 1966). Containing all variant readings of each text from first publication to *The Collected Plays of W. B. Yeats* (1952) as well as prefaces, introductions and notes published with the plays at various times.

Eric Domville (ed.), *A Concordance to the Plays of W. B. Yeats*, 2 vols (Ithaca: Cornell University, 1972). Invaluable in locating quotations and tracing the repeated use of words, phrases, images, and symbols through different plays.

George Brandon Saul, *Prolegomena to the Study of Yeats's Plays* (Philadelphia: University of Pennsylvania, 1958). Jeffares and Knowland (below) do not repeat all of his information.

A. Norman Jeffares and A. S. Knowland, *A Commentary on the Collected Plays of W. B. Yeats* (London: Macmillan, 1975). A compendium of information on production, publication, and interpretation of the plays. Obscure references and allusions are explained and critical assessments compared in controversial cases.

Klaus Peter Jochum, *W. B. Yeats: A Classified Bibliography of Criticism* (Chicago: University of Illinois, 1977). A useful guide to the published criticism of Yeats's work. See also the chapter on Yeats research in *Anglo-Irish Literature: A Review of Research* (New York: Modern Language Association, 1976).

Yeats and the Theatre

George Mills Harper, *The Mingling of Heaven and Earth: Yeats's Theory of Theatre* (Dublin: Dolmen, 1975). A brief and coherent summary of Yeats's views on the art of the drama. For the bulk of Yeats's collected writing on the theatre see *Explorations* (London: Macmillan, 1962).

James W. Flannery, *W. B. Yeats and the Idea of a Theatre* (London: Yale University, 1977). A study of Yeats's world-view and theory of drama as well as of his actual practice in the theatre against a wider background of European theatre at that time.

Liam Miller, *The Noble Drama of W. B. Yeats*, New Yeats papers, 13 (Dublin: Dolmen, 1977).

Andrew Parkin, *The Dramatic Imagination of W. B. Yeats* (Dublin: Gill & Macmillan, 1978).

Theatre History and Theory of Drama

Placing Yeats in context as a dramatist and man of the theatre is impossible without some understanding of the revolutionary forces at work in the European theatre around the turn of the century. Lyrical and imaginative forms of drama which relied on the development of anti-illusionistic production techniques contended with the absolute realism of Ibsen and his adherents. The art theatres which sprang up everywhere were often torn between those opposing modes. The political and social aspirations of a national theatre such as the Abbey tended to emphasise the conflict, and Yeats's drama should be seen against this background as well as that of theoretical questions such as the relation of dramatic representation to the life of a community.

Gerald Fay, The Abbey Theatre: Cradle of Genius (London: Hollis & Carter, 1958).

Katharine Worth, *The Irish Drama of Europe from Yeats to Beckett* (Atlantic Highlands, NJ: Humanities Press, 1978).

Ronald Gaskell, *Drama and Reality: The European Theatre since Ibsen* (London: Routledge, 1972).

Francis Furgusson, *The Idea of a Theatre* (New York: Doubleday, 1949).

Irish Myth and Legend

Isabella Augusta (Lady) Gregory, *Cuchulain of Muirthemne: The Story of the Men of the Red Branch of Ulster* (London: Murray, 1902). One of Yeats's principal sources and a synthetic narration in contemporary colloquial speech with little or no attempt to distinguish the authenticity of material taken from various sources or to retain the flavour and world-view of the originals. One might also wish to look at the companion volume, *Gods and Fighting Men*, along with her own plays, all of which are available in the 'Coole Edition' of the *Works of Lady Gregory* edited by T. R. Henn, 13 vols (London & New York: Oxford University, Gerard Cross, & C. Smythe, 1970-4).

Thomas Kinsella (trans.), *The Tain* (London: Oxford University, 1970). A very readable yet accurate translation of the central prose epic of the Ulster cycle as taken from the *Book of the Dun Cow* and the *Yellow Book of Lecan*. It contains stories not found in the *Book of Leinster* such as 'Exile of the Sons of Uisliu', 'How Cuchulain was Begotten' and 'The Death of Aoife's One Son', but not 'The Championship of Ulster', 'The Feast of Bricriu', 'The Only Jealousy of Emer', or 'The Death of Cuchulain'.

Cecile O'Rahilly (ed. and trans.), *Táin Bó Cúalnge from the Book of Leinster* (Dublin: Dublin Institute for Advanced Studies, 1967).

Japanese Nōh

Ernest Fenollosa and Ezra Pound (trans. and ed.), *'Noh' or Accomplishment: A Study of the Classical Stage of Japan* (London: Macmillan, 1916 [1917]). One of Yeats's principal sources.

Hiro Ishibashi, *Yeats and the Noh: Types of Japanese Beauty and Their Reflection in Yeats's Plays*, Yeats Centenary Papers 6 (Dublin: Dolmen, 1965 [1966]).

Richard Taylor, *The Drama of W. B. Yeats: Irish Myth and the Japanese Nō* (New Haven: Yale University, 1976).

The Critics

Excellent critical essays on individual plays have appeared in various journals from time to time and can be located easily in published bibliographies. The books listed below fall into three main categories. The first contains general considerations of all but a few of the plays. In every case there is an attempt to group works according to related subject matter, themes or forms, and dramatic techniques. Some interest is also shown in assessing characterisation and plot development along with the evolution of original dramatic forms and reliance on anti-illusionistic production methods.

Peter Ure, *Yeats the Playwright: A Commentary on Character and Design in the Major Plays* (London: Routledge, 1963; New York: Barnes & Noble, 1963).

Leonard E. Nathan, *The Tragic Drama of William Butler Yeats: Figures in a Dance* (New York: Columbia University, 1965).

John Reese Moore, *Masks of Love and Death: Yeats as Dramatist* (Ithaca: Cornell University, 1971).

The second category of critical work includes discussions of no more than five plays in any single case.

David R. Clark, *W. B. Yeats and the Theatre of Desolate Reality* (Dublin: Dolmen, 1965). Includes *Deirdre, The Dreaming of the Bones, The Words upon the Window-Pane*, and *Purgatory* as representative examples of different stages in Yeats's development.

Reg Skene, *The Cuchulain Plays of W. B. Yeats* (London: Macmillan, 1974).

Barton R. Friedman, *Adventures in the Deep of the Mind: The Cuchulain Cycle of W. B. Yeats* (Princeton: Princeton University, 1977).

The third category of criticism is characterised by concern for the more problematical middle and later plays, presenting theses which lead to an understanding of those works in terms of Yeats's religio-philosophical system or the esoteric and metaphysical traditions from which it springs. Because of the nature of some of the plays, especially within the Cuchulain cycle, this approach is used to some extent in works cited above, but here the method is dominant.

Helen Hennessy Vendler, *Yeats's Vision and the Later Plays* (Cambridge: Harvard University, 1963). A close consideration of *A Vision* and those plays which the author believes to be based upon its principles. Along with the early plays such works as *The Green Helmet, On Baile's Strand, The Hour-Glass,* and *The Unicorn from the Stars* are not dealt with, but less understandably, both *The Cat and the Moon* and· *The Herne's Egg* are also omitted. Another feature of the work is a tendency to interpret symbolic actions as images of creative or artistic processes.

Francis Alexander Charles Wilson, *W. B. Yeats and Tradition* (London: Methuen, 1958). An investigation of the esoteric and metaphysical traditions of many ages and cultures in an attempt to rationalise Yeats's system and his archetypal drama. *At the Hawk's Well, The Only Jealousy of Emer, The Cat and the Moon, Calvary,* and *The Dreaming of the Bones* are discussed.

Francis Alexander Charles Wilson, *Yeats's Iconography* (London:Methuen, 1960). An attempt to interpret the symbolism of the non-realistic late plays in terms of subjective tradition of religio-philosophical thought. *The King of the Great Clock Tower, A Full Moon in March, The Herne's Egg, Purgatory,* and *The Death of Cuchulain* are discussed.

Index

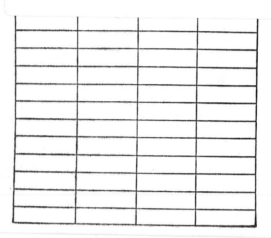